Your Life as Art

Other books by Robert Fritz:

The Path of Least Resistance

Creating

Corporate Tides

The Path of Least Resistance for Managers

Robert Fritz

Your Life as Art

NEWFANE PRESS
Vermont

Newfane Press
P.O. Box 189
Newfane, VT 05345

Ordering Information:
Contact: Newfane Press
(802) 348-7176

Printed in the United States of America

Library of Congress Cataloging-in-Publications Data
Fritz, Robert. 1943 —
Your Life As Art

Excerpts from "West Running Brook" from *The Poetry of Robert Frost* edited by Edward Connery Lathem. Copyright 1928, ©1969 by Henry Holt and Company, copyright 1956 by Robert Frost. Reprinted by permission of Henry Holt and Company, LLC.

Library of Congress Control Number: 2002114513
.
ISBN 0-9725536-0-6
1. Creative ability 2. Self-actualization (Psychology) 3. Self-help
4. Creative Process (Literary, artistic, etc.) I. Title

Cover design: Robert Jordan
Typeset by: Jennifer Thornton

First Edition January 2003

02   01   00   99   10   9   8   7   6   5   4   3   2   1

This book is dedicated to you, my wife, Rosalind.
Your beauty
both inner and outer,
touches my soul,
your penetrating mind and quick wit
captures my imagination,
your support moves me,
our life together makes me feel blessed.
You are poetry, music, light, color
and the essence of the most exquisite art there is.

A c k n o w l e d g e m e n t s

There are many people who have contributed their talents, insights, wisdom, and energy to this book. I am grateful to them all.

Thank you Jacques de Spoelberch, friend and literary agent for your untiring support of my work and books. Over the years, and through many book projects, your wisdom and mentorship has been a source of strength and light.

And thank you Charles Dorris, who served as the senior editor for this project. This is the third of my books your editorial coaching has guided. Thank you for helping me shape the book and refine my writing.

And thank you Norma Kelsey, friend and reader of the first draft. Your support and insight was critical and wonderful. Bravo.

And thank you Jennifer Thornton, for typesetting the book, and for your very helpful pointed suggestions.

And thank you Bill Brunelle for your extensive line edits.

And thank you Father Paul Wicker, you gave me just the right guidance and support. You are a friend, spiritual guide, and beloved colleague. Thank you Dr. Judith Boice for your invaluable contribution in the health section of this book.

Also I am grateful to you, Frank Newton, Lisa Delmar, and Rebecca Jarvis of the Robert Fritz, Inc. staff. Your dedication and untiring work on behalf of this book has been remarkable.

Thank you, Beth Massiano, for the research you did on behalf of the book. And thank you, Bruce Bodaken, for your challenges and insights. And thank you, Peter Senge, for your support, your originality, and your tireless work on behalf of a better world.

And I am grateful to you, Ivan, my son, for your support during this project. You helped on so many levels, from computer support, to ideas, to the kind of support a father really appreciates from a son, but has a little trouble being able to put in words.

And I am grateful to you, Rosalind, my beloved wife, who is the center of my life, friend, lover, colleague, partner, co-creator, co-discover, co-explorer. Our life together is the art that fills the pages of this book.

Contents

Introduction   1

Part One: Your Life Canvas   11

Chapter 1 · The Creative Process in Action   12

Chapter 2 · Lessons from the Painter   22

Part Two: Creating Your Life   35

Chapter 3 · True Love and Desire   36

Chapter 4 · A Look Deeper in   59

Chapter 5 · Frames of Reality   66

Chapter 6 · Action: The Road to Your Goals   76

Chapter 7 · Creating Your Life Long-Term   90

Chapter 8 · The One and Five Year Plan   110

Part Three: Structural Imprinting   127

Part 3 · Introduction   128

Chapter 9 · The Structural Patterns in Our Lives   129

Chapter 10 · The Conceptual Frame   156

Chapter 11 · The Structures of Our Lives   172

Chapter 12 · A Concept-Free Structure   182

Part Four: Artistry in Action   195

Chapter 13 · Vehicles For Your Life   196

Chapter 14 •Your Life as a Learner   199

Chapter 15 • Creating a Health Strategy   204

Chapter 16 • People   219

Chapter 17 • Creating Your Life as Art   227

About the Author   239

Your Life as Art

I n t r o d u c t i o n

The basic concept for this book is in the title. You can create your life in the same way an artist develops a work of art. When you begin to approach your life from that orientation, you transform your world. You become more directly involved in your own life building process, you create more of what you truly want, and you broaden the quality of your life experience.

You can *conceive* of the life you want to bring into being as an artist conceives of a painting, *take strategic actions* to build such a life as the artist takes all the necessary actions to create the painting, and *inhabit* the life you want to create as the artist may hang the painting on a wall to experience it.

Expressed another way, you can be the playwright, and *also* the lead actor, and *also* the audience for your own life play.

Your life can be your work, and you can be its author. And, like the artist, writer, playwright, filmmaker, and composer, the creative process can be your operational practice.

The Creative Process

The arts are a product of the creative process, which is the most successful process for accomplishment in history. And yet, most of us have not learned the fundamentals of the creative process, let alone mastered it enough to have it be the modus operandi for our lives.

But it makes sense to use the most effective approach there is. And that's what this book explores: how to use the creative process as the *major* modus operandi for your life.

You will learn how to think about what you want to create. You will learn how to understand your starting point, and how to create energy and momentum to use in the journey.

You will learn how to learn — from your mistakes and successes, from your experiences and the experiences of others. You will learn how to bring more of your life-spirit into your life. You will learn about time, about choice and about focus and about involvement. You will learn about using your own personal rhythms and patterns.

You will learn the basics of the creative process that include the mechanics, the orientation, and the spirit. You will have a chance to soul search, make critical life decisions, and evaluate yourself objectively and productively.

Lessons from the Arts

Ever since prehistoric people lived in caves and decorated their walls with paintings, the creative process has been an essential characteristic of human nature. Many say it is one of the elements of our nature that makes us human.

Neanderthal man and early modern humans lived during the same prehistoric period. In the debate anthropologists are having about the relationship between Neanderthal man and early modern humans, one of the differences that species experts sight as a point of distinction is art. The earliest Homo sapiens made art. Neanderthal man did not.

Throughout the history of civilization, there has always been art in its various forms. Every culture has painting, music, architecture, ideas about fashion, story telling, poetry, cuisine, and so on. Often the best part of a culture is found in its' arts. What defines a civilization? Yes, the politics, power structures, and institutions of control. But another force comes from those who create.

Often the arts and sciences remain as a legacy while everything else is forgotten. We don't think too much about Napoleon, but we still listen to Beethoven because he was able to reach something higher and more lasting. Not many, beyond the lofty halls of historians, think of the impact of Queen Elizabeth the First, but Shakespeare is still a force to be reckoned with, both as a playwright whose plays are always in production, and as a thinker whose words are still quoted, studied, and treasured.

You can create your life the way art is made. From this, you can reach new and better possibilities. Your life can grow to the quality and scope of the greatest art.

Calling Forth the Best in Us

Art often confronts truth, fundamental human conflicts, universal structural forms, questions of irony, questions of love and loss, questions of mortality.

Art has the ability to bring order out of chaos. Art has the ability to both involve us more deeply in life, and yet, at the same time, give us objective distance so we can see our world with greater perspective.

Art can also deal with the great mysteries of life. Yet, unlike philosophy, art approaches these mysteries quite differently. Rather than attempting to suggest answers to questions such as "why do we exist," or "where do we come from?" art reflects the quality of the unexplainable and the paradoxical. Art can explore both the human longing to connect with the broader Universe, and the profound limitation we have that denies the fulfillment of this longing.

That Certain Spark

Art comes in many forms, not all of it lofty and profound. One day I was surfing through the three hundred and sixty two channels we have on our television. First I stopped on CNN's report of bad news, then CNBC's report of bad news, and then FOX's version of bad news, and then three or four more. Then, suddenly, I clicked my remote and found a teenage dance program. Teenagers simply dancing to rock CD's. These were not the professional rock video diva dancers performing the elaborate choreography we see on MTV. These were a bunch of sweet kids dancing the best they could in their own way. The joy they had was more compelling and in a way just as true a report about the human condition as all the serious news the news networks were reporting that day.

The common pattern is this: as we get older, we tend to become more serious and stodgy. We tend to enjoy life less and less. We can lose touch with that spark we had when we were young (and what we often think of as "stupid.") As we get older, we can feel the pressures of greater financial responsibilities; greater health concerns; the feeling that the clock is running out; the feeling of the inevitably of things getting worse, either by getting worse, or by staying the same. And yet, instinctively we know there is more to us and to life than we often experience.

In Samuel Beckett's play *Krapp's Last Tape* an old man sits at a tape recorder and records an oral diary of the events of his life. He is a crotchety old man, bitter, critical, cynical, irreverent, and outrageous. As he records his comments into the recorder, we get a sense of the unpleasantness of his life.

At a particular point in the play, he begins to play some of the other tapes he has recorded throughout his life. We see the man as he once was, and we begin to understand why he has become the way he is.

One diary entry he plays is about a love relationship he had in his youth. We hear how tender and loving a person he once was, and how in love he was with a very special woman. After listening to the tape, the old man laughs at himself for being an absurd fool in his youth.

This is Krapp's last tape. He is about to die, and the tape he is recording is the last statement he will make about his life. In the dramatic climax of the play, he stops recording, takes the tape he had made as a young man in love, and plays it again. As he dies, he is holding on to the tape recorder playing his voice as the young man in love. As an old man, his cynicism had cut him off from life. But his most basic instinct was to hold on to life and love. His regret was not about his youthful foolishness of caring and hoping, but his wasted years of uninvolvement and isolation.

When you live your life as art, you open yourself to the spark you had when you were young. That spark you loved, that spark you may miss.

A play, and later a film that reflects this understanding so well is *Shirley Valentine*. The protagonist of this piece is Shirley Bradshaw, a middle-aged woman whose life has ground down to a very boring and conventional existence as a housewife in Northern England. Through flashbacks, we see the way Shirley was in her youth, a wonderfully iconoclastic rebel who had the ability to see through pretense and hypocrisy with great wit, humor, and irony. Shirley wonders how she lost the girl she once was. We see how, over time, the person she was drifted away.

At a critical point in the story, Shirley has a chance to visit Greece. Her husband, who himself has become more and more rigid and uninvolved with life as he has become older, can't understand Shirley at all. To add insult to injury, Shirley's daughter tells her that she is too old for adventures. And Shirley is almost convinced that her time has run out. But, at as the plot turns, she finally decides to go on a vacation to Greece.

There she begins to rediscover herself. The girl she was finally reaches true fruition as a woman. She regains the spark she had, and now it is able to be expressed more than ever as an adult.

If you don't stay in touch with your own spark, you can lose yourself. You can live quite nicely, move through life with ease, and have a sense that everything is going fairly well, and yet still feel the lack of something important.

Often people who feel something missing try to make up for it by looking for something outside themselves. Shopping, adventurous vacations, entertainment, and career ambition can be used as compensation. But those things never bring satisfaction for long. (By the way, I don't hold that there's anything wrong with enjoying shopping, adventurous vacations, etc. The point is that those things can't compensate for loss of spark.)

There is a way to reconnect with your essential nature. It is to create. One thing we can say about creators as a group is they seem to have a special x-factor that is generative. They are involved with their creations. As we become creators and our life becomes a work of art, we begin to have a direct experience of profound involvement and what we have been calling "spark."

Another Chance at Life

In Candice Carpenter's book, *Chapters*, she talks about the profound cycle of change a life can take. Often life does not travel in a straight line. Candice illustrates this point beautifully using a curved ascending line that suddenly curves around in a circle before it returns to the trajectory it had. The author, a brilliant business woman and corporate executive, was the co-founder of iVillage.com, ran emerging businesses at American Express, won an Emmy for a documentary series when she was a senior executive of Time Warner, and lived through many cycles of change. In *Chapters*, she describes one of the most common patterns people in transition experience. The first stage she calls *The Gig Is Up*.

This is when you know that what you have been doing is over. Perhaps you know it intuitively. Perhaps you know it consciously. But somehow you know it's over, and know it rather deeply. What had been your life can no longer go on. It is unsupportable on some fundamental level.

When you try to hold on to a job, career, relationship, living situation, or the direction your life has taken, and, to use Candice's phrase, "the gig is up," change will be thrust upon you with greater and greater force until you let go. The more you try to hold on, the more the intensity of the tornado that is pulling you out of the present unworkable situation.

The next stage in the pattern is *Falling*. Candice describes *Falling* this way: "disengaged, disidentified, and disenchanted, we fall into disorientation." This is the most frightening experience we feel in the cycle.

Then comes *A Walk In The Desert* in which you are able to reflect about the most existential issues of your life.

Next comes *Stirrings*. Candice describes it as: "All the threads of your past ultimately will be woven together as you become an accomplished creator."

This stage is followed by *A Stake in the Ground*, in which you begin to focus and then commit yourself to your new way of life.

Candice describes still more stages in the cycle that enable you to build your new life. There is much wisdom and truth in her observations about the nature of change. Change often is a kind of death followed by a resurrection.

To create something new, sometimes something old must end. This is the nature of the life building process. The *I Ching – the book of changes* describes this principle as molting, in which an animal drops its pelt or skin in order to grow for the new year. Change moves in rhythms. When we understand the rhythms that permeate the tempo of our life, we can, as musicians say, "play in the groove." When we are in the groove, everything works. When we are not in the groove, almost nothing works. This book will help you find your own life-rhythms, your own groove, the right pattern of change that is tailored perfectly to your own life.

When an artist finishes a painting, it is done. Next comes a new painting to create. This moment is the essence of *transcendence*. No matter what the past has been, we can begin again and have a fresh start. From the entrenched limiting pattern we may have been in, we are given new and wonderful possibilities. This is grace, a gift that allows us to go well beyond the past, and turn over a new leaf.

Your Generative Role

As a creator, your role is generative. You originate form and content that has it's own wonderful reason to be, it's own life, it's own purpose, and it's own intrinsic value.

Being a creator is a way to be involved with life at it's most basic and vital essence, it's deepest truth, it's richest expression. There is nothing better than being a creator.

Life itself is a creation, a work in progress, unfolding and revealing itself even as it is being created. We are part of that creation, and the mystery of the ultimate creative process permeates our lives with it's own rhythm, harmony, and lyricism. We are not always sensitive to the music, but the music is always there, ready to be heard. Not only that, we can add our own voice to it. We can move from passive audience to active performer in life's creative process.

You create anyway. You can't avoid it. If you shave, put on makeup, choose your own clothes, order food from a menu in a restaurant, drive, work at a job, have a family, and do most of the "normal" things that people do, you are making decisions that impact your life. You may not have thought of these acts as part of the creative process, but they are. As we delve more deeply into what it means to create your life as art, you will learn that the decisions you make are critical to the outcomes you can produce. The better you are at making strategic decisions, the better you will be at creating your life as an artist creates a work of art. You can move from inadvertently creating to consciously creating, from haphazard to deliberate.

Structural Dynamics

One of the most important discoveries I've made over the past twenty five years has to do with the realm of structure. Your life structures will determine your degree of success. The term structure has been used in many contexts in our lives, so a quick definition of how we will be using the term is in order.

Structure is a whole thing. A car is a structure. A rocking chair is a structure. A building is a structure, as is the human body. The first notion to understand about a structure is this: it is an entity that is undivided, complete, and total. Your life is a structure, and, as all structures, it will have certain ways it will act, behave, and work. Certainly a car works differently than a rocking chair. A building works very differently than does a human body. Your life may work very differently from how other people's lives work. Does your life structure work to your advantage, or does it somehow work against your best efforts?

There are two basic structural patterns people have: *advancing* and *oscillating*.

Advancing is a structure in which the success you have achieved becomes the platform for future success. You can build momentum over time, and the sum total of your life experiences leads you forward.

In an oscillating structure the success you have created is neutralized. A step forward is followed by a step backward. Within this structure, success cannot succeed long term.

If you try to change your life, and if you are in an oscillating structure, change will only be temporary. Each new possibility eventually leads to a reversal of fortune, and your best efforts are nullified. In *our* exploration of your life as art, we need to address the underlying structures you are in. We need to change them if they are self-defeating. We need to build new and better structures in order to advance.

Simply creating goals successfully is not the aim of this book. Many people can create important life goals, only later to lose the success they managed to create. You must learn how to keep the success, build upon it, and have it lead to further success over time.

And beyond goal creating, we need to explore the quality, spirit, and meaning of your life. We need to answer questions about freedom, control, identity, as well as aspirations and values. And we must examine what is true desire and what is not.

Three Legs of the Tripod

Art is made, not simply by the mechanics, but by the deeper orientation of the artist as well as the spirit. Artists do not work on single dimensions, and art does not work on single dimensions either. Think of your life having a counterpoint, with several themes going on at once. Works of art are not often perceived in the first viewing. Often the same work seems to change over time, and the viewer begins to see and understand new relationships, new perceptions, new meanings. Now these "new" discoveries came from the very same work, and the content for these new experiences were there all the time. The point: We don't always get it all at once. We need to spend time with art. Sometimes we grow in our perception because there is so much there, and we are only able to take in so much at a time. There are depths to you that are not always obvious at first glance. And as you delve more deeply into your life, you will find new discoveries, insights, values, aspirations, and depths that are so important to the final work of art that is you.

You need to learn the mechanics of the creative process, for if you don't, all your desires, hopes, and longings will have a low probability of being achieved. But you also need to reach for more than techniques. You need to find expression for the deepest and best aspects of your being. As you create, you learn, and as you learn, you grow in spirit and dimension.

The Four Sections of Your Life As Art

The book is divided into four distinct sections: *Your Life Canvas, Creating Your Life, Structural Imprinting,* and *Artistry in Action. Your Life Canvas* introduces the basic principles of the creative process and explores how to develop the mechanics, orientation, and spirit that can help you engage in your life-building process. The *Creating Your Life* section explores true desire and how we can structure our creative process around the most meaningful aspirations we have. *Structural Imprinting* explores the most critical issues there are in enabling us to make a shift from underlying structures that lead to defeating oscillating patterns, to true advancement and structural reinforcement. This section challenges some of our common notions about ourselves and the world we live in. *Artistry in Action* expands the creative process to include learning and creating health. It looks at how the people in our lives can be our environment, and explores how to understand the dynamics of our relationships.

Those readers who know my other books will find that some of the basic principles I have written about there are reviewed here. Even though you will find some ideas you have come to know, they are developed in new ways, expanded, and advanced. For those readers for whom this approach is new, you will be able to have enough foundation in the work that my colleagues and I have been exploring over the past thirty years.

Your Life as Art is an exploration of the life-building process through the very special understanding that creators have in their fields. If there's a better way to think about life, I haven't found it. The creative process fuses wisdom, spiritual depth, practical and strategic thought, learning, reaching, searching, discovery, imagination, structure, spontaneity, and passion into a total way of life that is rich with possibilities and experience. It is the most involving and exciting method by which to navigate life's currents. It is, at once, working with the forces of the universe and charting a course that is self-determined. It is a play of forces, some of which we control and many of which we do not. It is an adventure and a journey, a state of being and an unfoldment, human and Divine, timely and timeless.

Your Life Canvas

Chapter 1

The Creative Process
in Action

osalind and I host a television series called *Creating*. This program features guests who are masters of the creative process such as painters, composers, writers and filmmakers. Other guests create fantastic food and still others help people create well-being and health. One of the most interesting insights from these programs is that, while there is much common practice amongthese people, each creator has a very individual process for creating his or her work.

Some creators rely on improvisation and spontaneity; for example, painters Wolf Kahn, Susan Osgood, and Louise Jalbert. Other creators, such as clothing designer Louise Daoust, photographer Gilles Delisle, and conductor Ewan Edwards, use an approach that allows spontaneity, but within the context of a clear definitive idea for the form and vision they have. The great poster artist Vittorio Fiorucci talks about the creative process as an act of assembly. Performers counter tenor Daniel Taylor and pianist Alain Lefevre see their creative process as an extension of the music they perform so the audience can be touched by the deepest expression of the composers' compositions. Emmy Award winning screenwriter Ernest Kinoy (*Roots* and Gore Vidal's *Abe Lincoln*) talks about his years of experience in developing his craft and the special moments in which something unexplainable happens. Author Peter Moore Smith (*Raveling*) talks about his writing schedule. He writes from 7 am to 9 am every day of the week. Author Charles Sigismund (*Champions of Silicon Valley*) interviewed the major technology pioneers (Netscape's and Silicon Graphics' Jim Clark, Yahoo!'s Tim Koogle, etc.) and found that clarity of vision and the ability to invent a means to serve that vision was central to each of these creators.

We found that generally the creators who work over extended periods of time (writing a novel or screenplay, producing a film, composing an opera, developing a business, and so on) use a more structured and formal creative process. Those who create over a shorter time frame (landscape painting, sketching, writing a poem or a song, and so on) used a less formal process, and use more spontaneity and improvisation. The longer and more complex the creation, the more structured and formal the process. The shorter the timeframe and scope, the less formal the demands of the process.

In your life, you have both short and long term objectives. The overall direction of your life tends to be a long term creation. Therefore, a more formal and structured process is necessary to succeed. Spontaneity and improvisation better serve some aspects of the quality of your life. As we explore your life as art, we need to develop the skills of improvisation and the discipline of form and structure. These seemingly opposite approaches actually feed each other to the enrichment of both. If you tend to be a very methodical person, a little whimsy now and then won't hurt you. If you are the kind of person who is impulsive, impromptu, and instinctive, a little structure won't kill your free spirit. It will only enhance that wonderful spirit by giving it focus and direction.

Consequently, creating one's life as art is an individual journey for each of us. You cannot follow a formula. There aren't any set rules. You need to create your own process of development. You need to create your own creative process—one that will work especially well for you.

While there aren't rules to follow, there are principles you can use in your tool kit. Think of these principles as the common practices that most creators embrace in their work. Some of these principles fall into actual *mechanics* of the creative process. Other principles are about your *orientation* as a creator. Still other principles are about the guiding *spirit* that sparks the direction you take.

In music, rhythm, melody, and harmony are inseparable in reality. When we listen to music, we hear rhythm and melody and harmony as an indivisible aural experience. But composers are able to separate these factors when they write music. They can create rhythmic motifs one moment, then think about harmonic content, and later still, construct melodies, themes, and counterpoint. The result appears in reality as one unified experience, but creating that impact comes from the composer separating each of the components.

In a similar way, the mechanics, orientation, and spirit of the creative process are inseparable in their impact, but we can develop them separately as we begin to compose our lives. Each factor must be developed well in order to bring the full power of the creative process to bear on your life.

The Mechanics:
Smart Design / Good Execution

The mechanics of the creative process fall into two major categories: *design* and *execution*.

It is hard to build a house or a building without the blueprints to guide the construction teams' actions. Without proper design, we can work against ourselves, waste energy and effort, and become entrenched in unworkable conditions. Our design can be strategic or organic.

If we have longer term goals and aspirations, the better choice is strategic. The test of a good strategy is this: because you've taken certain steps, it is easier to take further steps.

A good strategy often begins with easier steps that can generate a quick start, followed by more involved steps that deepen and broaden the project, followed by more complex steps that enable us to do those things that would have been highly unlikely or even impossible before the earlier steps were taken. So, begin with easy-to-take steps and let them lead to more involved, complicated ones.

Sometimes an organic approach is more suitable for the result we are after. In an organic process, one thing naturally leads to another.

A good example of organic development is the typical farmhouse. When the farm family built their house, at first it was small, perhaps a front room, a bedroom and a kitchen. As the family grew, new rooms were added to the house. These rooms were connected to the original house, but they didn't look the same as the house. More kids came, and soon the house was growing with more added rooms and more added rooms. Sometimes the house would grow and finally connect with the barn.

We find these types of houses all over North America where land was plentiful. They have a wonderful beauty to them, and one can imagine the life of the families as the houses grew and grew.

Some lives are like these farmhouses. One thing leads to another, and over time a life is built. While this is organic development, it is not mindless development. There is conscious thought, decisions, building, discipline, work, and commitment expressed in every stage of growth.

The difference between strategic and organic development within the creative process has to do with the timeframe. What are your aspirations? If they are focused on long-term accomplishments, you'll need to be strategic. If they are focused on the quality of your life, perhaps an organic approach will serve you well.

An example of the difference between the need for a strategic approach over an organic one is found in city planning. Recently I gave a talk to a group of city planners. They were discussing the growth of their respective cities. Some of them were experiencing very fast growth that was putting pressure on all the cities systems, such as water and electricity supply. An organic approach would lead to chaos in a very short time. Inadequate systems limit the potential for proper growth, and burden all of the existing systems. This is why city planners are so needed these days. They are able to take a strategic overview and help design public policy that can best serve the entire community. So, while the organic approach toward development works very well for the farm family, it cannot be translated into more complex issues of city design.

In our own lives, some aspirations require a clear strategy. We cannot reach our goals if we are not designing a comprehensive approach. Sometimes, an organic approach is better. We make a meal, take a weekend trip to the country, crack a joke, write an e-mail, decorate a room, take a photograph. In these cases, capriciousness may be the order of the day.

Organic and strategic thought is a matter of design. The best design in the world is useless unless we act upon it. Many people make plans but don't follow through.

The Critical Role of Action
in the Creative Process

Often people plan but don't act because they think the plan must be perfect before they act. They become paralyzed by the concept of perfection. In the practical life of creators, adequate is adequate. Imperfect plans make films, build buildings, produce technology, market products, grow gardens, and even fly rockets to the moon.

Planning is often needed, but so is action. Often the time to act is before the plan is fully developed. This is because your first actions put you in touch with the real world. Action and planning form a feedback system. You make the first draft of your plans; you then take some initial steps which, in turn, give you new insight about how practical your plans are. Are the assumptions built into the plan true? If not, you will have to change your plans accordingly.

Action, even if you are going in the wrong direction, can create momentum. If you are in motion you can more easily change your direction than if you are standing still. So, take action. Even if the actions aren't leading you directly to your goals, they will generate energy.

To design and execute a plan, you must develop many skills including:

- The skill of forming goals and developing vision.
- The skill of evaluating your current situation.
- The skill of developing the right strategies and tactics.
- The skill of using feedback to adjust actions.
- The skill of generating momentum and traction.

Each of these skills will be explored further in this book. Each one is essential to the mechanics of the creative process. Together, these skills enable you to develop and master your own personal creative process.

The Orientation: Where You Live

Over the years one of the biggest discoveries we have made is that a person's orientation counts. What does the word mean in the context of the creative process? One way of describing orientation is where we live.

Let's say that we had high ambition, but somewhere in our psyche we also had a deep-seated fear that if we succeeded something bad would happen. Many people have the impression that good things come with a price tag, and if they succeed in something important, there will be a counter impact that will cause them trouble or loss. When things are good, some people become a little nervous. A friend of mine would say in these types of situations, "It's so good ya can't stand it!"

This person lives in a world with its own rules, one of which is *don't be too successful or you'll get it in the neck*. This is an example of an orientation in which success is felt not to be a good thing exactly, because it may cause unintended negative consequences. The result: The person will go after important goals but will secretly fear accomplishing the goals.

This is only one of many examples of orientation. We will explore issues of orientation later in this book, but for now, understand that the right mechanics and spirit coupled with an unsuitable orientation will not succeed, even if you initially reach your goals. You must understand your current orientation, and if it's unsuitable for creating, change it.

Freedom from Circumstances

As people master their own creative process and begin to apply it to their own lives, one of the major shifts of orientation they experience is from reacting or responding to circumstances, to being generative and independent of those circumstances.

We are taught that circumstances are the power in our lives, and that we should just learn how to deal with them. Questions about what matters to you are irrelevant if you only can respond to your circumstances in which you find yourself. Those who have rejected the idea that there is a proper response to learn are left with rebelling and reacting. In our society, you are thought to have progressed if you move from reacting to responding. However, in each case the circumstances are still the dominant factor in your life.

In a generative or creative orientation, circumstances are not the dominant force. You are. Yes, the circumstances are a factor in your creative process, but they are only your starting point. You need to understand them in the same way you need to know where you are in any journey. If you are traveling to New York, how useful is it to know your starting point is Boston? How could you get to New York if you were in Boston but thought you were in Atlanta?

This shift from a circumstantial to a generative orientation is essential if your want to create your life as art. It's popular these days to be a victim of circumstances. There are those whose entire adult lives center around how they were victimized as children.

While many people have suffered tragic pasts, not everyone who has is limited by the past. I know people who live in constant rage about the abuses they suffered as children. They can't move on. They seem trapped. Do they want to be? No. But they can't live the lives they want from within the victim orientation. Yet they can learn how to go beyond the past and live in the present. This is often a truly disorienting change, because the unresolved issue they are hoping to resolve will still go on unresolved. The events of the past will always be the events of the past. As Dr. William Glasser, the psychiatrist who developed *Reality Therapy and Choice Theory* has said many times, "You can't learn how to fulfill your needs by reviewing examples of how you weren't able to do that in the past."

When such comments are made, people who are in a victim orientation often feel profoundly misunderstood, unjustly wronged, and unheard. They need to know that it is not lack of compassion about their past that is in question. If we could wave a magic wand and undo the terrible events we would. But the past is the past. And the past is over. Now is the only moment you have in which to create a new future.

Mwalimu Musheshe, the executive chairman of the Uganda Rural Development and Training Program was imprisoned and tortured under the Ugandan dictator Obote because Musheshe supported freedom and democracy. One night, his guards tried to sneak him out of his cell to kill him. The other prisoners got wind of the plot and began to shout his name. Then they began to riot until Musheshe was led back to his cell, bruised and beaten, but alive. After years in prison, Musheshe was released when Obote was overthrown. He went on to dedicate his life to building his country, not as a politician, but as a leader in rural development. I knew Musheshe for many years before I learned what he had suffered under Obote. I had noticed deep scars on his face, but, in a way, I hadn't really noticed them because of his beautiful smile, his joyous manner, his open heart, and his infectious laugh. When I heard about his life in prison, I was not surprised on one level, having known something about Uganda's recent past. But on another level, it was hard to put together Musheshe's past with his way of being. When I heard the story (not from him, incidentally) my thoughts were immediate and involuntary: "This is a great man."

Our friend Andrée Jalbert was given a death sentence a few years ago. Cancer. She tried to make the most of her life, and she did as much as she could. But then came the inevitable. Rosalind and I were with her in the hospital the day before she died. She knew she was dying, and yet she still had her wit and humor and zest for life. "Can we do anything for you?" we asked. "Yes," she whispered. We came close. "Get me out of this!" she said in a full voice. And then she laughed and then we laughed, even as we held back the tears. This dying woman was still hitting her stride and wasn't going to let a little thing like death curve her spirit. Her ex-husband came to visit her. He was moved and uncontrollably emotional. He began to cry. "Do me a favor," Andrée said to him. "Yes?" he said. "Save it for the funeral." In the hospital, Andrée did as much to comfort those who came to say goodbye as they did for her. We saw her for the last time on the day she died. She was at peace, ready to move on, and still living life fully until the final moment.

There is a dynamic urge toward life even in the most dire of circumstances. How can we understand the likes of Mwalimu Musheshe and Andrée Jalbert except to observe that human beings have the capacity to go well beyond the circumstances and create something extraordinary.

Sometimes people live in the past, not because of their suffering, but because of their victories. Biff, the son in Arthur Miller's classic play *Death of a Salesman*, was the high school football star. But he had not lived up to his grand beginnings. His father Willy Loman also lived in his son's past glories even as he tired to ignore Biff's present failure. Loman was a tragic figure who lived in his own past glories, real and imagined. One of the saddest elements of the play is his inability to live in reality and the dark consequences of that fatal flaw.

Time has a way of moving, and then moving again whether you want it to or not. Soon today becomes the past. You can't hold on. Yet the creative process is a fact of the current moment. You can't go back in the past and create. And while you can prepare for the future now, you can't reach into the future and create. The creative process happens in real time. The orientation that is needed is one in which we can live in the present.

The Spirit: A Deeper Look

The third dimension of the creative process concerns the deepest aspects of the human being. Often, this realm is thought of as the domain of philosophy, metaphysics, or religion. But, there is another lens with which to view this aspect of the human makeup, one without the limitations of beliefs, dogma, creed, doctrine, or conviction. This lens explores without an idea of what one might find. This true exploration can open the door to the deepest source of the creative process. For your life to be art, you cannot ignore your own depth, your own reservoir of vitality. Through the creative process, your true spirit and essence is expressed throughout your life. When you are in touch with this spirit, you are transformed in many ways. It impacts your life direction, your understanding of what's most important to you, and your quality of life. It can be a platform from which to stand, a touchstone for deepest values and highest aspirations, a source of inner strength, and a fountainhead for amazing intrinsic generative energy.

The nature of creating is that we connect with the deeper spirit of ourselves throughout the process. While, often, the experience of this spirit is spontaneous and inadvertent, the connection can be developed consciously. Your deeper spirit can have a dominant place in your life, which will enrich you in the most incredible ways.

Most of us sense there are dimensions of ourselves that are just below the surface, but, nonetheless, strive for expression. When we are not able to find a place for these aspects of ourselves, we feel that something is missing. And, something is. As we explore this aspect of your life as art, you will be challenged to find this depth that is personal to you. The experience you reach may surprise you, delight you, enlighten you, open you, expand you, and touch you.

The Three Aspects of Creating

Each area, *the mechanics, the orientation,* and *the spirit,* needs exploration and development. The three, together, are inextricably tied. You can master the mechanics of the creative process and yet not have a suitable orientation or spirit, and you will find that you are only going through the motions of the process. The outcomes will not capture the height and depth of your true desires.

You may have the most favorable orientation, but if you do not know the mechanics, you will not be able to accomplish much.

You can have the spirit, but an unsuitable orientation or lack of mastery of the mechanics will frustrate you because the deeper calling of your spirit is unable to manifest its innate wisdom in the real world.

In the next chapter we learn vital lessons from the painter, including how the mechanics, orientation, and spirit of the creative process take on form and structure. The chapter focuses on the most powerful dynamic there is within the creative process.

Lessons from the Painter

As we've said, not all creators follow the same path, and not all disciplines are identical. The writer's process is different in many ways from the composer's process. The filmmaker's process is still different from that of the inventor or software engineer. Your process will be different from mine, different from your friends', and different from anyone else's.

But before you are left on a desert island like an Outward Bound participant on the first solo overnight survival training, you can use a little background to help prepare you. The Outward Bound soloists first have very useful training in how to survive alone in the wilderness before they begin their adventure, and so should you.

While there are no rules to follow, there are principles to understand. When you know the operational principles of anything, you can begin to make up your own rules, and even change those rules when it makes sense.

One of the best ways to quickly explore the major principles of the creative process is by thinking about how painters work. Painters use every principle that you need to understand to create your life as art.

Creating Your Vision

For a moment, imagine yourself as a painter, and your life as the painting you are creating.

You're standing in the center of your studio. It is quiet , and the northern light coming through your window is gentle, perfect, soft, filling. In front of you is the blank canvas; on your right, the paints on your palette. Your assorted brushes are organized by size and type. You can smell the sharp edge of the paint, you can hear the silence, and you are alone. You are ready.

So now what?

Now you are ready to answer the very first question in the creative process: *What do I want to create?*

This question generates a decision. You will begin in your mind's eye. You picture something. Perhaps a still life, a face, a scene from a sports event, a landscape. (Often painters are very clear about the image they are trying to reproduce on the canvas.) Or perhaps what you picture has more to do with color and texture rather than specific image. (Some painters are less concerned with the actual likeness of a painting, and more interested in the abstract expression of its visual impact.)

Whether representational or abstract, you, as painter, have something in mind. The principle you will use in creating your life as art is this: have an idea in mind about the result you want. What kind of life do you want to build?

Sketching the Life You Want

Some people have a flash of insight. They suddenly know exactly what they want. Their clarity of vision is as lucid in the beginning as it is at the end of the process. This is very rare, especially when the creation is a person's life.

More often than not, ideas begin as little seeds, and then grow to a full vision of the result you desire. The vision of the outcome develops gradually over time. The more you are involved with developing your ideas, the more you will get to know them.

One way painters develop their ideas is through sketching. Before they begin to work on the full and final canvas, they often do many sketches to learn more and more about their vision. As you begin to develop your ideas about your life, you can conduct little experiments similar to an artist making sketches. Perhaps you want to develop a career as a fashion photographer. One thing you may do is take classes with professionals. Another is to practice shooting friends as if they were doing a fashion spread. You may ask the local dress shop if you could shoot their latest displays. Each action you take tests the waters, practicing, gaining experience, and further getting to know the life experiences you want. Each action is like making a sketch to study the vision you are developing.

Or perhaps you want to live in France. Rather than pulling up stakes and making the big move, take vacations there. Learn French and join a French club where people speak the language. Study the culture, history, job market, cost of living, and so on. You are getting to know more about your idea by trying it on for size. You are sketching. Let the vision develop and build. With each experiment or sketch, your understanding of the outcome you want will deepen.

In describing her process of developing an idea for a painting, Artist Janet Fish said, "I am very interested in finding out what I actually see. I don't really know until I get going."

From sketches and studies, the vision crystallizes in the painter's mind. In a similar way, you will develop the vision of the life you want to create more and more over time. While it may come in a flash, more often that is not the case. You will get part of the idea, and then another part, and then you will begin to see how the parts fit together, and then, later still, you will begin to have a comprehensive vision of the life you want.

Learning About the Vision

Painters often develop their ideas by building their vision in stages. In a similar way, the vision you have for your life may be built in stages.

Painter William Beckman said, "If I did a painting of you right now, the third or fourth drawing would probably be stronger than the first because I would get to know your face better each time I did it."

Through sketches and drawings, the artist is studying his or her vision. The vision often develops over time and experience, rather than comes in one moment of inspiration.

There's a famous Michelangelo story about his great masterpiece, the sculpture *David*. Michelangelo was chipping away at an enormous block of marble one day. Someone, who was watching him work, stopped the great master to ask him how he knew just where to chip away. "Inside this marble is *David*," Michelangelo is reported to have said, "and I'm just releasing the *David* that's in the marble."

The point that is attempted to be made by this story is that the creative process is a matter of eliminating the non-essentials. If you were to use this idea, you would strip away everything that wasn't essential to your life. This version of the creative process assumes that the vision exists in some perfect state and our job is to discover it. That is a very different notion than inventing the vision. While a vision may sometimes come in a flash, most often it develops, grows, migrates, and matures.

Let's change the scene. Instead of Michelangelo, it's Beethoven. One day he is sitting at a table with an enormous piece of black paper in front of him. In his hands he has a bottle of White Out. He puts dabs of White Out on the black paper. A visitor asks the great maestro what he is doing. "I'm releasing the *Ninth Symphony*," Beethoven announces.

The fact is that the Michelangelo story is fiction. That's not how he developed his vision for this great masterpiece. What's missing in the story about Michelangelo chipping away everything that wasn't *David* is the fact that Michelangelo made various sketches of *David* before he began to sculpt the final statue. The story also ignores the smaller statues of *David* Michelangelo made before he created the final and largest one.

Michelangelo had gone through the same process that other artists go through, that of developing a vision over time and experience. His talent was supported by a practical work strategy that allowed ideas to grow as part of the overall process. More often than not, you will find yourself inventing your vision rather than discovering a vision. Just as the painter makes sketches and does studies of the final result, you may want to sketch out your ideas and study various aspects of the final vision. *Form many different pictures that illustrate the final look and feel of your vision.*

The Vision as Guide

Painters always have the vision in mind when they work. They cannot afford to get lost in the details or lose sight of the vision in other ways, because if they do, they will make wrong moves that can destroy a painting. The vision is a constant guide and target. It is the object that is aimed for, and the standard by which progress is measured.

For painters, the vision is both in the back of their minds and in the forefront of their focus. Likewise, when you create your life as art, your vision will be in the back of your mind. But also, you will at times focus directly on the vision with laser-like intensity. This will enable you to generate energy and increase your self-motivation.

The Power of Tension

We're back in your studio and you now have a vision for your painting, or at least enough of one to enable you to start. What do you do next?

You look at your blank canvas. It is white and empty. While you look at it, you begin to imagine the painting you envisioned on the canvas. As you do this, you are establishing one of the most important dynamics in the creative process — *tension*.

The word tension in this context doesn't mean pressure, anxiety, stress or strain. Rather, it describes a relationship in which one element of a structure is *contrasted* by another element of the same structure. The first element is the vision of the completed painting. The second element is the current state of that painting, at this point, a blank canvas.

The tension is a force or dynamic that generates energy and movement. Tension seeks resolution. Tension evokes change from a situation in which something is *different* or *discrepant* from something else, to one in which the difference has been eliminated, and both elements are now the same.

In the beginning of the process, the canvas is different from your vision of the painting. At the end of the process, the actual canvas is the same as your vision for the painting. This is the moment in the process when the painter signs the painting, an act that declares, "This painting is the same as my vision for this painting."

In the beginning of our creative process there is a contrast between our desired state (our vision of the outcome we want to create) and our current situation (where we are now in relationship to that outcome.) If we are successful, at the end of the creative process the desired state and the current state are the same, ending the contrast and resolving the tension.

An example of a tension-resolution system we all experience is hunger. The tension is formed by the contrasting relationship of two elements: the amount of food the body desires; and the actual amount of food the body has. This difference generates a tendency for behavior: to eat. And the natural tendency when we are hungry is to eat until the tension is resolved, which happens when the desired amount and the actual amount of food are the same.

In the arts, tension is the major dynamic that moves a piece forward. Think of the dramatic contrast between the hero of the film and the villain. In music, direction and movement are created by contrasts such as loud-soft, high pitch -low pitch, rhythmically active-inactive, and densely textured -sparsely textured. In painting, contrasts include light-dark, bright-dull, and warm colors-cool colors. Creators of all kinds learn to use contrast and discrepancy in their creative process. The major contrast they use is between their vision of the final result, and the current state of the project. When they do this, not only are they setting up a tension, *they are setting up a structure.*

How Structure Determines Behavior

Part of your job in creating your life as art is to set up structures that support the process. Structure is one of the most powerful influences there is on the way you live your life and your probability of success. But the word *structure* is greatly misunderstood.

Partly that's because the word *structure* is used in so many different contexts with so many different meanings. But when we are precise about its meaning, we begin to address the *dynamics* of structure — what it is, how it works, why it works the ways it does. So here's a working definition of structure:

> Structure is an entity…a whole thing…a construct.
> The first idea we can have about structure is that
> there is an organized unity to it. A structure is single rather than plural. Yet within this single whole
> entity there are parts. These parts can be called
> elements or factors of the structure. These parts
> have a special relationship to each other. They are
> connected and they impact the other elements of
> the structure.

Here's a quick example from the classic film *Casablanca* of how the parts of a structure affect each other.

The plot of the movie involves a love triangle. Two men (Rick and Victor) love the same woman (Ilsa.) She, in turn, loves both of them.

This is a wonderfully dramatic conflict (for a movie that is,) and we, as audience, want to know how the plot will resolve. Will she end up with Rick? Will she end up with Victor? What will happen to the one who loses? How will she decide? What will she do with the love she has for the one she will leave? The tension resolves in the climax of the film in one of the most famous and loved scenes from any movie ever made, as the question of who Ilsa will end up with is answered. And the structure of the plot is so strong, that even though I have seen this film at least four hundred times, each new time I see the film I think that maybe this time Ilsa will stay in Casablanca with Rick rather then get on the plane to Lisbon with Victor.

In the first part of the film, Rick is at his bar Rick's Café American. We understand many things about him: he is a loner, he is a reformed alcoholic, he is sad and mysterious (after all, he is played by Humphrey Bogart.)

Into his bar walks Ilsa and Victor.

The film heats up when Rick is asked to join their party, and it is obvious he and Ilsa have been lovers in the past.

Here is a situation in which each character has impact on the others, and so, if we eliminated one of them, the structure would change, and their behavior would also change.

Imagine that Rick is at Rick's Café American one night, and in walks Ilsa...*without* Victor. Does that change the tendency for behavior? You bet. (After all, Ingrid Bergman plays Ilsa.)

Now imagine that Rick is at Rick's Café American one night, and in walks Victor...without Ilsa. Does that change the tendency for behavior? Of course.

Now imagine that Ilsa and Victor have come to Rick's Café American, but Rick had left for New York a month earlier. Does that change the tendency for behavior? Yes.

So, the elements of a structure have a special relationship with each other, and if they are changed, the structure itself is changed.

Some structures are very suitable to the creative process, and some are not. As we will see throughout this book, the right intentions, aspirations, visions, and values within the wrong structure will lead to an oscillating pattern in which first you may achieve your goal, but later, lose it as the pendulum swings. One important dimension of the creative process is setting up structures that can lead to full and irreversible success. When this lesson is applied to your life, your chances of success go up dramatically.

So the tension you will be using in creating your life as art is structural — in other words, *structural tension*.

Structural tension is the best and most powerful structure there is in the creative process. One of your jobs in creating your life as art is to establish and manage structural tension throughout your creative process by developing the ability to envision the result and observe the present situation in relationship to that result.

Painters use this ability constantly, managing two distinct data points, the painting in their vision and the painting on their canvas. This is one of the keys to creating your life as art, holding two pictures in your mind at once, the desired state of your life viewed against the actual state of your life.

Like an archer pulling back the arrow, straining the bow, we can aim structural tension toward our chosen goals. The archer understands the principle of tension and learns to master it. Tension precedes release. Before we let the arrow go we establish critical tension so that our action will have the greatest chance of reaching its target.

With structural tension, you can accomplish the most amazing things. With it, you have an engine that can help propel you, like the arrow leaving the bow, toward your goals. With structural tension, you are working *with* the forces of nature rather than against them. With structural tension, you can build a pattern in which success succeeds and builds upon itself.

Establishing Structural Tension

On the level of mechanics, you can establish structural tension by taking two actions: defining the results, objectives, goals, and outcomes you want to achieve; and then observing the current situation in relationship to your vision.

Doing this takes two types of skills: *envisioning the results you want; and evaluating your current reality objectively.* These skills can be developed by practice, and we will explore ways to develop these skills later in this book.

The mechanics of the creative process are essential. And so are the *orientation* and the *spirit*.

On the level of orientation, *structural tension is a way of life, not just a form you are using.*

Orientation is a way of describing where you spend most of your time. Another thought is: where do you live, or how do you live? If structural tension was your main address, you would live in a place in which you clearly see your vision, and your current circumstances. Not only would you have this clarity on occasion, but as a constant awareness.

For the painter, structural tension is not only a mechanical technique, but also a way of life that is deeply integrated within them. Like a surfer catching the perfect wave, or a glider pilot navigating perfect airwaves, painters "ride" structural tension during their creative process. Structural tension is internalized and assimilated into their consciousness. The more deeply internalized, the more they are able to negotiate the currents.

The mechanical adoption of structural tension is very effective. Over the years we have worked with tens of thousands of individuals, and thousands of organizations, and we have seen the great success created by knowing the goal, tracking current reality, and organizing strategic actions accordingly. This elementary use of structural tension is a good start. While there is more to creating than the mechanics, the mechanics are not to be underestimated. They are an important fundamental to your creative process. And as you begin to internalize structural tension, the mechanics and the orientation feed each other as you move toward mastering your creative process.

Good mechanics are great, but more is available! As you begin to internalize the vision and current reality, structural tension becomes a more powerful dynamic force in your life. Your actions become more and more motivated and you become more and more inventive about your process. Your creativity and talents flower. It seems as if your whole being is aligned and working together on behalf of the full manifestation of the vision. Structural tension is becoming central to your orientation. And often there is something extra that begins to happen.

Internalizing Structural Tension and the Extra-Normal

Another thing that happens is a little hard to explain. There is an almost mystical dimension to the impact internalized structural tension can have. Coincidences begin to occur regularly. You find just the right opportunity to accelerate your progress. You read an article in a magazine you hardly ever read, and right there is the exact piece of information you need to supercharge your action plan. You get invited to a party, and there you meet someone who is just the right person to help you with your idea. Things begin to fall into place as if the universe were on your side, helping to move you toward your goals.

These types of events are illogical from a purely rational and material point of view. But, no matter how skeptical you may be about the idea that something extra-normal can happen, it will happen anyway. This phenomenon is so common that most people have an abundance of stories that confirm the experience. When structural tension is internalized, strange and wonderful things can happen that help you create your vision.

While this is a common experience, extra-normal events, by themselves, are not enough to create the results you want. For more involved goals, hard work, learning, skill, competence, talent, energy, thoughtful decision-making, careful evaluation, strategic adjustments, and a host of other practical activities are essential to your success.

If all you did were to sit home and focus on structural tension, you would not achieve many of your most important goals. But, isn't it nice to know that in addition to taking all of these types of actions, you get a "little extra help" to increase your chances of success on many more dimensions than simply mechanical.

If these types of extra-normal episodes begin to happen to you when you are internalizing structural tension, one word of caution is in order. *Do not glorify the experience.* If you do, you will begin to shift your focus from the creative process to something else.

Process is only as good as the results it serves. Process should never be exalted, dramatized, celebrated, exaggerated, or blown out of proportion. The only test of a good process is how effective it is within your value system. A good process may include extra-normal as well as normal means, and all that really counts is how well the process worked to help you create your goals.

I have seen many people fall into the trap of magical thinking followed by becoming progressively superstitious when they began to glorify the extra-normal experiences that happen to them. They became less and less practical, and more and more symbolic and metaphorical. Reality as a critical data point loses it's actual significance, and instead of evaluating reality objectively, it is interpreted, given psychic meaning, made into a sign, a symbol, and an omen.

If you were a painter, and you had internalized structural tension, you may have many extra-normal experiences during the painting process. Little "accidents" may create an effect better than one you could have consciously invented. The light may suddenly hit the face you are painting in a way that is more dramatic and interesting than your first impression. Paint may have spilled in just the right way to reinforce the expressive quality you were trying to achieve. These extra-normal events simply become part of the entire process. You're glad when they occur, but you can't base your entire career on them. You do not glorify them, but you do welcome them as another aspect of your working strategy. *What matters is how well you can use everything that is available to you for creating your life, not the process you are using.*

Sleep on it

For many creators, sleeping and dreaming is a place to further the creative process. Once structural tension has been internalized, your subconscious mind begins to resolve the tension you have established. When I am working over an extended period of time writing a piece of music or an article for a magazine, or developing a program idea for a television series, or working on a book, I often get ideas and answer critical questions during the night.

I never have a notebook by my bed as some people do. (There's noting wrong with that, of course.) I have trained my mind to remember the insight. I may have a dream, or a thought. I may roll over, be half-awake for a moment, and have a sudden realization. When I awake in the morning, the insight that my sleeping state produced is pretty clear.

If, within the first four or five hours after arising, I do something with the new idea, it will stick. If I don't, it will drift away. But, I have found that if the idea drifts away, and the structural tension is still a dynamic force seeking resolution, the idea will come back, perhaps the next night, perhaps from a comment someone says, perhaps while watching TV. I don't have to hold onto the nighttime insights tightly as if they are in short supply. They will be there when I need them, as they always are.

The Spirit

The mechanics and orientation are two legs of the tripod. The third is the spirit. The spirit of structural tension comes from two of the most powerful forces there are in life: Love and truth.

The reason you create a result that you care about is that you love it enough to see it exist. This type of love is not simply responsive love. In responsive love the situation comes first, and the love second. You meet, you fall in love.

Creators love their creations before the creation exists. As Robert Frost said about poetry, "A poem begins with a lump in the throat." The painter loves the painting before there is a painting. The filmmaker loves the film before the principle shooting takes place and before the actors are hired. The composer loves the music before it is ever performed. The type of love an artist experiences during the creative process is generative rather than responsive.

Artists usually don't talk about the spirit of love they have for the work they are creating. For one thing, it's hard to talk about, and for another, it's such a normal and ordinary experience that, while it is special, it is very common.

Love takes many forms, not all of them inspired. Love is a state of being in which many experiences exist. The generative love an artist experiences is there on good days and bad, in times of ease and times of frustration, in moments of victory and moments of defeat. Generative love is a constant throughout the entire process.

The spirit of creating your life as art evokes this type of generative love. As you manage the mechanics and deepen the orientation, you are simultaneously in a state of love that fills you with great resolve and passion.

The other force the spirit of structural tension engenders is truth. While we picture the results we want, we also honestly and objectively see the current conditions we have. Artists are often tough as nails when it comes to observing reality. They cannot distort reality by making it better or worse than it is. If they did, they would not get the feedback they need to make adjustments to their process. Painters do not lie to themselves about the current state of the painting. They see it with almost clinical objectivity. People who do not know many painters are often surprised by how uncompromising painters are in their truthfulness about their work.

Truth of this kind is a matter of mechanics in that artists need accurate feedback. It's also partly a matter of orientation in that they value truth because they want to know exactly what is the reality of their work. And there is a spirit to truth, which is so beautifully expressed in the phrase, "truth for truth's sake."

The spirit of structural tension is generative love and truth for truth's sake. What could be more magnificent within humanity?

Creating Your Life

C h a p t e r   3

True Love and Desire

She floats toward the camera, wearing the trendy swimsuit, her skin — tan, soft, young, healthy. With her seductively knowing eyes and effortless accessibility, she seems to whisper "Yes, yes, yes!" She is the quintessence of glamour and sex appeal. What are they selling? Perhaps a new designer perfume. Perhaps a trip to a Caribbean resort. Perhaps auto insurance.

What they're really selling is an image of desire. Not so much *what* we desire but *how* we desire. In this image, desire is about *seeing* and *wanting*. Desire comes in a flash. It is rooted in temptation, the forbidden fruit, the instant and compulsive *need* followed by the quick lunge toward instant and compulsive *gratification*.

Marketers come by this notion honestly. They only have 30 or 60 seconds to get our attention. Who could blame them for wanting to dazzle us so they can make their pitch?

For the record, I think those types of ads are great fun, but I can't say they work well on me. I might watch the ad, especially if it has a good music track, but I hardly ever know what they're selling. And I think most of us have the same impression.

Through these types of *Ad Age* images, desire becomes a strange icon. It's too bad, for desire is such a good thing.

How can you get where you want to go if you don't know where you want to go? Goals are born of desire. We need to be in touch with our real desires to form our goals.

I know that there are those who advocate living a goal-less life. Go with the flow, be spontaneous, give up attachments, fly by the seat...And, for some people, that's a good idea. Some people can drift from experience to experience and enjoy the ride. Sometimes these people talk about the trip itself as the goal. Getting somewhere, no matter where it is, is the goal.

This is the image we get from Jack Kerouac's great book *On The Road*, in which the protagonist travels and observes and finds life in its many and varied phases. But Kerouac couldn't have written his book using this same freebag approach to life that his fictional anti-hero does. First he had to have a desire, *the book*. So while we, as audience, can live in the experiences he described in *On The Road*, he used a different process for creating the book. Step one for Kerouac, as it is for most creators, was establishing his goal, based on his desire for the book that he envisioned.

The fact is we want things. We are programmed to have desires. Sometimes the things we want are very simple and immediate: food, enjoyment, a good laugh, a good night's sleep. Sometimes they are longer term: building a business, building a family, building a home, building a career.

Some of the things we want are in reaction to circumstances: having a headache go away, being able to pay the bills this months, making the plane on time, filing the tax return by April 15th.

For some people their most immediate desires are not about what they want, but about what they don't want—what they want to avoid. Instead of their desires being the organizing force in their lives, the problems, obstacles, and difficulties are.

Your desires are important because they can be the central theme that organizes your actions. Without real desire, it is hard to create because there is little motivation to get involved.

Waiting for Your "IT" in Shining Armor

What is desire?

On a basic level it is a want. The prime condition of human nature is to want things. We want to live, so we therefore want air, food, and warmth. We have desires that are generated by simple appetites, and we have desires that are generated by pure altruism and love of others. We have both simple and more complex desires that come in the form of ambition, greed or charity, kindness or a sense of higher calling.

What we need to know is this: *Not all desires are created equal.*

Some desires can be the firm foundation of the life building process while other desires can be the quicksand that leads to destruction, decay, and disappointment.

The desires that help us build our lives are self-generated. That is to say that they are *independent* from the circumstances in which we find ourselves.

These types of desires could rightfully be called *true desires* because they are not circumstantially formed but come from something deeper and more essential in us. They are not cut from the same cloth as the *seeing and wanting* type of desires. Sometimes when leading workshops in which the subject is creating one's life, I ask people this question: "How many of you know what you want?"

Usually about a third to a half of the people raise their hands. "And how many of you do not know what you want?" the rest of the group raises its hands. That's at least half and sometimes two-thirds of the people in the group who seem not to know what they want. Could the percentage really be that high?

In fact, it isn't really that high once we begin to explore what true desire is. In the end, almost everyone is able to connect with his or her true desires. So why is it hard for some people at first to answer the first and most basic question of the creative process: What do you want to create? i.e. what do you desire?

Many people make the mistake of thinking if they find the "right" thing to want, they will find the key to success, happiness and satisfaction. For these people, it almost doesn't matter what the object of their desire is, as long as wanting this thing "works." And by works, they mean that it motivates, propels, inspires, and stimulates them into action, which in turn leads them to victory.

The basic flaw in their thinking is orientational. They think that something outside themselves can "do it for them." They often have the subliminal impression that somewhere in the world is a magic key, and this key unlocks a door through which they can pass. Sometimes I like to call this "the IT in shining armor." And, like the maiden who sings, "Some day my prince will come…" this person can almost hear, "Some day my IT will come," which will take him or her to the Promised Land.

If you actually thought that something outside yourself could change your life, give you purpose, give you direction, energy, and momentum, of course you would set off on a mission to find that special something. Who wouldn't?

The trouble is that this *something* isn't there. It's a mirage. It doesn't exist.

Nothing outside yourself, in and of *itself*, can make you happy.

So, if you're looking for that right IT in shining armor, you will have a long wait.

People sometimes think that money can make them happy. Years ago a friend took me to an Amway meeting. The speaker began to ask people this question: "What are your dreams?" The group easily answered. "A yacht!" "An island off of Florida!" "A mansion!" "Financial independence!" The speaker wrote these answers on a flipchart and then circled them.

"And how are you going to afford your dreams?" the speaker asked. He then made the case that the way to afford the dreams was to sell Amway products.

Now, I'm not against people making money selling Amway. I am against supporting the illusion that somehow money will fulfill your true desires. While there is nothing wrong with having financial goals, and nothing wrong with being rich beyond your wildest dreams, don't expect realizing that goal will bring you happiness. If it did, there would be fewer unhappy rich people. Notice that many lottery winners who are thrust into sudden wealth often suffer more than they benefit. (Many studies have been done that make this point).

There are very happy rich people, but their riches are not the essence of their happiness. Something else is.

And the notion that "something outside myself can make me happy" is not limited to money. For some people it's "finding their life's work." The notion is that there is something they're supposed to do. And it's not just anything, it is very deeply important work that, once found, will bring them profound satisfaction. So these people search and search but never find their "life's work" because the notion that this work is out there is an illusion. It is another IT in shining armor.

The Internal It

There is a variation on "something *outside* myself..." and this is "something *inside* myself, which when found, will make me happy." This internal thing functions exactly as if it were external. The form is the same: Feel incomplete, presume that there is something that needs to be found, search for it and hope to find it. Usually the pattern includes finding many candidates, which at first may look pretty good, but turn out to be disappointing in the end.

For the people who seek their desires internally, there are many approaches and worldviews that suggest what should be found: religion, psychological experiences, and ideas about discipline or self-denial. But as you search for a candidate, you find that this IT isn't it after all. Then you begin to question your own judgment. You become indecisive. You feel more and more insecure and lost. But even as this happens, you still feel that just around the corner is this IT...this wonderful IT. But what corner?

Some people go in the opposite direction of our friends at Amway, and instead of asking "What are your dreams?" they say, "Give up your dreams. Be unattached. Don't want anything. Be desireless."

This idea is rather simple. If you think the root of suffering is desire, then, if you give up desire, you would no longer suffer. Of course, the irony is that the desire to give up desire is a desire. Also, the hoped for consequences of the act, overcoming suffering, reaching spiritual fulfillment, etc, are themselves desires.

To try to "find" the right desire is the wrong approach in creating your life as art. You won't find it. You can't build your life around it. You will simply fall into the trap of being indecisive.

The "right" desire isn't out there, or "in there" for that matter. This fact isn't something personal. It is the nature of desire itself.

True Desire Versus Choice

Have you every tried to love someone you didn't love? It didn't work, did it? No matter how much you might want to love someone you don't love, the fact is that you don't love that person. There are many things about the creative process that center around the power of choice. Love happens not to be one of them.

If you could choose whom to love, there would never be unrequited love. We would only choose to love those who loved us back.

We do not choose who or what we love. True desire is a form of love. And in a similar way, we don't choose what we desire.

We may or may not be aware of what we desire, but one thing we can't do is manufacture desire. And just as we can't force ourselves to love people we don't love, we can't force ourselves to want what we don't want.

The converse is also true. We can't not love what we love, and we can't not desire what we desire. We either have a desire, or we don't. End of story.

Once we understand our desires, we may make choices around them, but the desire itself is not the subject of choice. You want what you want because that is what you want. And it's hard to organize your choices around things that you don't care about, or that at least don't lead to things you don't care about.

If we really understood the true nature of desire, would we waste time trying to find it? No. Would we waste time trying to stamp it out? No.

Here's another point to add to the picture. If you thought you needed to find what it was you desire, and you went on a search and find mission, *the true desires you actually have would become invisible to you*. How could you recognize your true desires if you applied the IT in shinning armor standard of measurement to them? You wouldn't. Your true desires might be right in front of you, but you would not recognize them because you would be looking for an erroneous ideal.

Knowing what you want isn't a revelation that suddenly opens the door to success, happiness, victory, or anything else. It is simply an understanding about what's most important to you. You may decide to organize your life around your true desires or not, but at least you will know what you want on some deeper level.

Don't give desire the wrong job. Its job is not what *it* can do for *you*. It's rather more a factor of what *you* can do for *it*. It's not an IT in shinning armor for you. You are an IT for your desires.

If you haven't organized your life around your true desires, I recommend that you do. Let them become the foundation for your life-building process.

Fleeting Passion Versus True Desire

Today, people talk about passion in very confusing ways. "Find what you're passionate about!" oft comes the advice. "Put passion in your life and in your work!" we hear espoused. "Find your passion!" is preached. "Follow your passion!" is proclaimed. The way passion is talked about, one gets the impression that passion is something that is found, adopted, and followed. The way the word is expressed suggests a state of excitement that thrills and electrifies us with rapture and inspiration. Passion, in this context, is about emotion, fire, animation and feeling.

This type of passion, like inspiration, is a temporary phenomenon. As all artists know, inspiration and passion have their moments, and then the moment passes. What do you do on days you are not inspired, if you only can feed off of inspiration? What do you do on days that you are not in the throes of passion, if you only can respond to passion?

In creating our life as art, one thing we can learn from artists, writers, composers, choreographers, and filmmakers is this: Inspiration comes in rare moments, and the creative process is not about inspiration.

Creators know very well how to work on the many, many days when they are not inspired nor filled with passion. *The source of their motivation to create doesn't come from any particular experience they happen to be having, but from the true desire to bring a work to com - pletion.*

The advice to "follow your passion" fails on days when the passion passes.

And it must be remembered that following your passion sometimes can lead to terrible results — think of crimes of passion. And crimes of passion are seen as a type of temporary insanity that explains why an otherwise rational person does something simply awful.

Passion is not an essential factor in true desire. At least not when it is described as a type of emotional or inspirational response.

I say these things as a person for whom passion is essential. Let me tell you some of the things that I'm passionate about to see if I can make an important distinction between the temporary fit of passion we can experience, and another kind of passion we, as human beings, have in abundance. This second type of passion is more a state of being which does not easily pass, as does an inspirational or emotional response.

I am passionate about music. I always have been. I can remember a conversation when I was about nine-years-old with some chums in front of Riley's Drug Store in our town, and we were talking about music. My friends said something like, "Music? Ugh!" and, "You like Muuu-sick? Weird!" And I said, "Yeah, I love music." This was not the manly thing to say to my fellow nine-year-olds, but I didn't care. It seemed so obvious to me that music was a good thing, and if it was or wasn't cool, it didn't matter…I loved it anyway. This is my first memory of taking a position that didn't agree with what anyone else was saying.

I have always loved music, and I must admit I have no idea why.

Years later when I was learning to become a composer, my composition teacher at the Boston Conservatory asked me this fascinating question: "Why do you want to write music?" I thought about it, and I gave the truthful answer: "I don't know." "Well, Mr. Fritz," he said with that intensely critical eye he could put on, the one that would go right through you, "you better find out."

For years I thought I'd better find out. I had an abundance of theories about why I wrote music, none of which made sense to me. But after years of pondering this question, I finally found that the answer is still I don't know why I want to write music. And, I don't need to know.

The impression my composition teacher had given me was that I somehow had to know why I wrote music. At first I thought that if I knew I would write better. But, in the end, how does one explain love? You can't, not really. You love because you love, not because of other things.

How well Elizabeth Barrett Browning captured this idea, first in a series of letters Robert and Elizabeth Barret Browning wrote to each other, and then in a poem that Elizabeth wrote in her *Sonnets of the Portuguese*.

In a letter from Robert to Elizabeth dated October 23rd, 1845:

"…I love you because I love you…"

And Elizabeth back to Robert October 24th, 1845:

"I...thought that you cared for me only because your chivalry touched them (my infirmities) with a silver sound – and that, without them, you would pass by on the other side."

And in another letter dated May 11th, 1846 she wrote Robert:

"There is no good reason for loving me...But if there is to be any sort of reason, why one is as welcome as another...you may love me for my shoes, if you like it...except that they wear out."

And the sonnet develops this point further:

> If thou must love me, let it be for nought
> Except for love's sake only. Do not say
> 'I love her for her smile...her look...her way
> Of speaking gently,...for a trick of thought
> That falls in well with mine, and certes brought
> A sense of pleasant ease on such a day' —
> For these things in themselves, Beloved, may
> Be changed, or changed for thee, — and love, so wrought,
> May be unwrought so. Neither love me for
> Thine own dear pity's wiping my cheeks dry, —
> A creature might forget to weep, who bore
> Thy comfort long, and lose thy love thereby!
> But love me for love's sake, that evermore
> Thou may'st love on, through love's eternity.

Love for love's sake only. What truth is expressed in these lines. Truth that is as true for true desire as it is for true love. Yet this passion is on the level of a state of being rather than a momentary inspiration or emotional experience. This is passion that lasts, that does not change when feelings change, that transcends the shifting circumstances in which we might find ourselves.

Another thing I have passion for is talent. When a singer, writer, filmmaker, comic, painter, poet, musician, conductor, actor, dancer, and on and on, performs, I thrill to that person's talent. I can't explain why. I could never be a film critic or any other type of critic because I have nothing but praise for the creative act performed by talented people. And there is such an abundance of talent around today.

As far as I'm concerned, these people are kind of saints. Not of the cloth, but of the soul. And if God had a church of artists, he would point to each one of them and say, "This is one of my blessed children of whom I am proud."

And I am passionate about my family. My beloved wife Rosalind, my son Ivan, my daughter Eve—they are so remarkable. Noone has to tell me to love them. I don't need to *find* the profound depth of love I have for them. I couldn't write a mission statement and say anything rational to explain how or why I feel as I do for them. It is beyond words. But it is not beyond knowing and experiencing, and what I know is that every single day I am deeply grateful that they are in my life.

Your passion is not an affect. It is not a response. It is not "catching fire." It is simply there if it's there. And if you place no demands on it, such as casting it in the role of savior, you can get to know it. But you need to look in the right place and in the right way.

The Dynamic Urge

You've made a vow to eat a healthy diet, and you have gotten through the first few days of your resolve pretty well. You've avoided eating the cookies that your friendly neighbor has brought over, you managed to order a salad with sliced cold chicken breast at lunch, the same lunch that everyone else was having the meatball grinder special. You drank Pellegrino water instead of beer during the Superbowl party. You lost 3 pounds, and you feel stronger, taller, better looking. You are even starting to take pride in your strength of character.

But then, disaster strikes. You pass a McDonalds. The smell of hot grease drifts into the car. You begin to think about a Big Mac with fries. You decide not to give in. You don't. You drive three miles. But then, up ahead, look. It's a sign…a symbol. About a half-mile up on the right, two golden arches stand in grand relief from the horizon. One thing you can say about the civilized world, there is always another McDonalds within three miles. The golden arches beckon to you. "You've done a good job," it seems to say. "You deserve a break today." You seem guided by your nose.

More tantalizing smells of hot grease fill you with desire. More images of a Big Mac and those wonderful slim tasty fries. You begin to hear yourself think that having a little treat once in a while won't hurt anything. Balance is the key to life, isn't it? A long famine of cold breast of chicken, and short feast of grease, white flour, sugar, starch, salt.

In the moment it takes to have this thought, you find that your car has driven up to the drive-through window, and your voice seems to be ordering TWO Big Macs and extra large fries. Once the food is in the car, you have to eat it. Think of all those starving kids that this will help.

We are human beings, and so we have this funny thing about us. We are inconsistent. We seem to want one thing one moment and something entirely different the next. For the most part, people are convinced that they shouldn't be inconsistent. Being inconsistent means you are a flake, a hypocrite, a weak-willed impotent nincompoop. But the fact is we are inconsistent.

Sometimes this doesn't matter. So what if sometimes we like rock and other times we listen to classical? So what if sometimes we want to see the latest cinematic epic, and other times we are in the mood for a romantic comedy? Variety is the spice of life, it is said, and our ability to enjoy many different experiences is a stroke of luck.

But when it comes to creating our lives, inconsistency can be a scourge to our plans. We can't gorge on McDonalds in the middle of our health regime.

How are we to understand our shifting desires?

Some desires are not really desires at all, but are products of a person's compensating strategies. Let's say that you had the belief that you were worthless. You may then develop the need to create a sense of worth. And, once this counterbalancing ideal of creating worth becomes a factor, you may want to do things you think are worthwhile.

Because of the structure, and the compensations that it generates, you may experience desire—in this case the desire to be a worthwhile person. Perhaps you begin to do volunteer work, or you contribute to worthwhile charities, or you spend time with a friend in need. These actions may seem motivated by a desire to help. But it is not a true desire; rather it is a synthetic desire that is generated by the structure itself.

The test of a true desire is that it is self-generated. It is not a product of anything external. A true desire is independent from the circumstances you happen to be in. You would still have this desire, even if the circumstances changed. I have given the name *Dynamic Urge* to describe the human trait of having desires that are a product of the person, him or herself, and not an outcome of anything else.

Within the dynamic urge, desire comes in different forms or frames. The best way to describe these frames is to imagine a video camera. If the video camera were shooting an extreme close-up, details would fill the screen. If we moved the camera back to what's known as a medium shot, we would see shapes and patterns and understand the relationship of elements to each other within the picture. If we backed up even further to an extreme long shot, we would lose any sense of detail and perhaps not even know what we were looking at.

Think of these three different types of camera positions as a way of framing what we are considering.

The Close-up Frame: Instincts and Impulses

Using this metaphor, the extreme close-up shot on the level of dynamic urge is appetites, instincts, and impulses.

> appetites, instincts, impulses

We all know people whose lives are organized around their appetites or their impulses. Rosalind and I once knew a very large English gentleman whose whole life centered on good food and wine. He was a neighbor and we were fortunate enough to be invited to the many feasts he held. He served the most delicious roasts, fowl, fish, along with exotic side dishes and outlandish deserts. Of course, all of this was washed down with the best wines from his extensive cellar.

Did I mention the guy was large? He was over three hundred pounds. One day, after one of his typical banquets, he began to tell Rosalind and I that his doctor had warned him to cut out his food and wine pattern. He was also warned to quit smoking. He said he couldn't bring himself to do this yet. But then he went on to say that his doctor told him his life was in danger if he didn't change his ways. He was in his mid-thirties, and yet he had the look of someone much older. His focus on short-term gratification of his appetites was more dominant than his long-term hope for a long and healthy life.

For someone who is focused on appetites, impulses, and instincts, time moves in short episodes, and thoughts of longer-range time frames are hard to conceive.

Recently I saw a very sad documentary featuring teenage street kids that illustrates this point. Many of these teenagers had AIDS, were involved with drugs and prostitution, didn't eat well, and didn't have a place to sleep. When asked about the future, none of them thought they had a future. Most of them couldn't imagine themselves living past age twenty. For these kids, time passed quickly and was very compressed. Their lives were about appetites and impulses, and the notion of something more long range seemed inconceivable. Without a longer time horizon, these tragic young people had little motivation to change their destructive habits.

In this close-up view of the dynamic urge, desire calls for quick gratification. Those things that cannot be resolved quickly are hard to accomplish. In terms of structural tension, the person cannot tolerate ongoing states of discrepancy between longer-range goals and the current situation relative to those goals. Therefore, the person is unable to support longer-term projects. A person who is focused from the vantage point of a close-up cannot easily build a business, compose a symphony, direct a film, develop a product, manage a team of people, grow a garden, or write a novel. Projects that demand sustained development over time are not within these people's natural reach.

But we can change the frame. As a camera can move from a close-up to a medium shot, we can back up, see from a broader vantage point, and the dynamic urge is refocused. What becomes dominant within the dynamic urge are two of the most important factors that can shape our lives as creators. They are aspirations and values.

The Medium Frame: Aspirations and Values

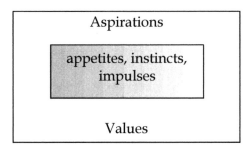

As we back up to a medium shot, our sense of time broadens. We can conceive in longer time frames: weeks, months, years, decades and even beyond. Our highest aspirations often take time to create and maintain. Not only was Rome not built in a day, neither are careers, organizations, mastery of various skills, and even relationships. When people have a low tolerance for living with structural tension, and they have a high need to gratify desires immediately, they cannot even begin to think in terms of aspirations that need time to develop. But, as we begin to consider longer-term objectives, we are able to appreciate the fact that many good things take time, and we are motivated to *take* the time they need. We are not tempted toward quick gratification that would not serve creating our goals.

Aspirations

A problem for many educators is that they are teaching subjects that are not useful to the students at the time they are being taught. If students are in a close-up frame within the dynamic urge, they will think that what is being taught is irrelevant to their lives. Not only that, but the learning process unfolds over time, which does not lend itself to quick gratification of desire.

The best way to work with these students is to help them move from a close-up to a medium shot within the frames of the dynamic urge. They can refocus their desires on longer-term aspirations. This can be taught and encouraged by asking the student to think, not in days or weeks, but months and years. This type of activity is more than simply asking the question, "What do you want to do with your life?" Rather it is a true exploration in which the student is able to consider time from a longer vantage point. From this perspective, they will see their true aspirations. Once they understand that some of their goals take time and effort, they are motivated to act on behalf of those objectives over extended periods of time.

Sometimes people say of such a transformation, "He has woken up," or, "She's a late bloomer." Students, after being uninvolved with their lives, are suddenly engaged wholeheartedly in the process of learning what they need to learn so they can support their aspirations.

Values

Values are another aspect of the medium shot within the dynamic urge. Values are one of the most important organizing principles in life.

What are values? Values may include such qualities as truth, justice, and kindness. They may also include comfort, fun, avoidance of conflict, and involvement.

How do we know our values? We know them when they are in conflict with other values. Values are relational. The word denotes measurement. In art school, student painters conduct something called "values studies." These are pictures that are painted in one color, perhaps blue or sepia. In a values study, the student is testing the relationship between light and dark, because the gradations between light and dark give the illusion of three dimensionality on a two dimensional plane. The student is learning to determine what's predominant and what's subdominant.

In a similar way, that's what we do when we determine what's more important and what's less important. For example, imagine you had two values, one truth and the other kindness, and you went to visit your sick grandmother on her deathbed. For you, truth may be the higher value and you may say, "Gee, Granny, you look terrible." Or perhaps kindness is the value that is more important to you in this situation and you say, "Gee, Granny, you look great." By choosing what you say, you are determining the value that is senior to you and the value that is junior to you. When values are in conflict, as they often are, you need to make a choice. If you don't, what you may find yourself saying is, "Gee, Granny, for a dying woman, you sure look great!"

Within the dynamic urge, values are not formed by the situation, even though various situations may have different competing values that become hierarchically important within the context of the situation. Both truth and kindness may be values you have. These values would be internally generated. No one would have to teach you them.

Typical of the notion that values can be taught, teacher and musician Norma Kelsey has said, "In Fredrick County schools where I taught for over twenty years, there is a program called "Character Counts." All the local politicians are on the bandwagon with this. Teaching honesty, caring, etc., etc., became the duty of *all* teachers. Of course, it's such nonsense. Kids have their own good values!"

Teaching values, recently a glitzy political theme, can't be done. So, while the candidate for office declares, "We need to teach our kids family values!" the fact is that our children form their own values. Most often, they have very good values. *What they need to learn is how to use their true values as a basis for making deci - sions.*

Let's adjust our political candidate's talking point to say, "We need to teach our kids how to organize their lives around their *own* values!" While this doesn't sound as good on the stump, and our candidate may lose the election by a landslide, at least our politician was honest.

Your highest aspirations and deepest values are your truest desires. When you act in ways that are inconsistent with them, you can feel as if you are not being true to yourself.

The medium shot of the dynamic urge is the most powerful vantage point from which to organize your life. And while Rome and the fulfillment of your aspirations are not outcomes you can build in a day, you will be on the right road.

The Long Frame: Vague Hopes and Longings

If we back up the camera to the long shot, we find the focus becomes soft and fuzzy. It's hard to make out what we're looking at. In the frame of the dynamic urge, we have entered the land of vague hopes and longings.

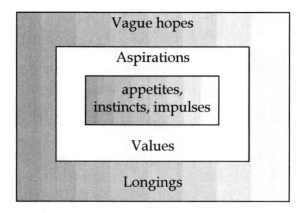

We all know people who have vague hopes about what they will do someday — write the great novel, travel to Tahiti and paint, invent a computer program that will transform the way we understand mathematics, move to the country to live the simple life.

Time, for these people, is very long indeed. So long that their goals are in a distant future. So long that they have trouble organizing around these notions. And the hopes and longings are so unclear that they don't exactly know what they want.

These longings are real. But they are not focused enough. It is hard to aim for these targets because they are too far away.

Changing Frames: A Matter of Choice

Happily, we can change the frame. If you move from vague hopes and longings to aspirations and values, you suddenly have something to create.

Here are some tips that can help you change the frame:

• Change the time frame. Instead of the amorphous someday, begin to conceive of goals that can be accomplished in weeks and months.

• See this first episode of creating these goals as practice. So pick goals that are relatively easy, within your reach, and have a series of steps that demonstrate your progress.

• Pick results you want, but ones that are not the most important goals in your life. While you're practicing, take the pressure off.

When you begin to create, what if you don't know what you want? Simple. *Think small*.

Everyone wants many things, including small things—a dinner party with friends, a newly decorated room, a weekend trip to a theme park, a tomato plant that provides fresh tomatoes all through the summer.

Here's some advice for those of you who have had the IT in shining armor complex and who seem not to be able to think about what you want. Because you have considered goals from the standpoint of return on investment (what it will do for you) you don't know the simple pleasures of wanting something for its own sake. Before you begin to consider your highest aspirations, consider less ambitious ones. Remember the old story of the guy who comes to New York City sometime during the 1940's, and is trying to find Carnegie Hall. He is lost, so he stops a man on the street. The man, as it turns out, happens to be the great conductor Arturo Toscanini. "Excuse me, sir. How do you get to Carnegie Hall?" asked the visitor. "Practice!" answered the great maestro, "Practice!"

If you're not in the habit of thinking about what you want, practice before you attempt a full performance. There are things you want. But they are not always the biggest things in the world. Often people have an image that what they want must be grand, important, significant, profound, and glorious. If this is the case, rid yourself of this impression. There may be desires you have that are not in the category of the greatest things a human being can want.

If that's a *true* desire, you never have to look for it. It will be there, and you can't miss it. If you are on a search-and-find mission for the big objective, you have already entered the realm of the purely idealistic and fictitious. You are terribly misguided because you think that what you want has to have a particular scope to it. You are measuring what you want based on the wrong standard. You are not connecting with true desire, but on the *image* of what you think you *should* want.

If this is the case, let me save you years of frustration, disappointment, and failure. GIVE IT UP! Stop trying to find your grandiose desires, and begin to lower your sights until you can see the real, true desires you have. Stop looking for your life's work or where destiny is supposed to lead you. Stop looking for desires that will bring meaning to your life.

Start small with those things you know you *actually* want. And you will begin to get an experience of what it's like to create something you actually want. Many such experiences will give you a growing instinct about how true desire works.

This instinct will put you in good stead when you begin to consider some of the longer-range aspirations you have in your life. But only after a period of practice and experience, are you ready to explore broader territory.

You won't have the old illusions that your aspirations are IT(s) you must find that will do it for you. Rather, you will find those goals that actually matter deeply to you, not for what they will do for you, but for what you can bring to them.

You love what you love because that's what you love. You desire what you desire because that's what you desire. And you have a choice to organize your life around your loves and desires, or not.

Choice means you can do it or not do it. So if you choose to have your true desires become the centerpiece of your life, it is a road you have picked, not one you have to take. There are no guarantees, no assurances of happiness or satisfaction. Just the experience that you are taking the right path, a path that finally rings true.

All of life is moving, striving, on a quest to advance forward in time. This is the profound dynamic in which life is asserting itself to unfold and manifest its own existence. Desire is the human expression of that dynamic. It is the creative spark, a Divine gift in which the heart and soul can envision beyond the moment to an unfolding universe of previously unimagined possibilities. It is the soul and spirit of the creative process. It is truly yours. No one can give it to you, and no one can take it away from you. But, sometimes, we seem to take it away from ourselves.

Bringing Your Life Spirit into Your Life

In Carol King's classic song *You've Got A Friend* there's one of those killer lines that stays with you throughout your life, and here's the line:

They'll take your soul if you let them,
But don't you let them, no, no.

There is so much in our lives that seems to dull our life spirit. We can feel that our soul has been taken, or at least we have to drive it underground for it to survive.

One reason for this is that our society demands conformity on some very basic levels. There are good reasons for us to learn how to get along, make adjustments to accommodate others, and function within the fabric of the community. But, we cannot let society, others in our lives, or our own fears and complacency cloud the most interesting and vital aspect of our makeup—our true spirit.

Your true spirit is alive and well and waiting for modes of expression. It is a latent part of your dynamic urge. It strives for a voice.

Your spirit is free, wonderful, good, kind, and just. And it also has a dash of demon in it as well. It is the saint and the leprechaun. It is the greatness that can soar to the highest heights, and the little tease who loves to point out that the Emperor has no clothes. It is naughty and nice, cool and hot, sweet and sour, fast as the speed of lightning and patient as a Zen master prompting a slow student to move toward enlightenment. It is your inner wisdom, your teacher, your guiding light, your friend, your touchstone for truth, your nobility, and your ally. And the question is this: does it have a place in your life?

If it doesn't, you will feel a degree removed from yourself. You may feel inauthentic, slightly lost, disconnected, and vanquished.

How could your life be art if the spirit was missing? It would be like food without flavor, touch without sensation, a joke without a punch line.

In John Frankenheimer's film *The Manchurian Candidate*, the Lawrence Harvey character is unlovable, stiff, neurotic, and tragic. And yet, in one of the most poignant moments ever recorded on film, he tells the Frank Sinatra character about the one time in his life when he liked himself. It was when he was in love, and he was transformed. In spite of his character traits, he was able to reach his truest spirit. Although throughout his life he had been a very narrow person, his real spirit was just below the surface, striving for expression, which burst forth when he found himself in love.

Because of this scene, we, as audience, began to care about him as a character. Before this moment, he was simply a dramatic enigma that the Sinatra character needed to solve.

You don't need to develop this spirit. You need to give it a home. Let it live in you, thrive in you, fill you with that which is best in you.

In the arts, we see creators put their spirit into their work. The more it is there, the more a personal expression we feel. The film director Frank Capra (*Mr. Smith Goes to Washington, Meet John Doe, It Happened One Night,* and his Christmas Classic *It's a Wonderful Life*) had a moment in his life in which he saw that he had the power to express the most important content that could be expressed within his films. But he feared he would corrupt his art if he began to "send messages." He was at the top of his profession, had just won an Academy Award for best picture and himself for best director, and he was offered the best contract any director had ever had up to that point. But he felt that his deeper spirit wasn't able to be expressed, and he was in doubt how to do it. In a conversation with Max Winslow, he said:

> "I don't give a damn whether you listen, or whether you think it's corny. But directors have the power to speak to hundreds of millions for two hours, and in the dark. Okay. But this director doesn't know what the hell to say. Am I going to give up entertainment and bore people stiff with 'message' films?…Well, what am I supposed to preach to people for two hours and in the dark? God, country, brotherhood, mother love? Jesus! They're tired old clichés."

And Winslow replied,

> "Well, well, well! You're growing up—a little. But you've got a long way to go. Many great plays and books have been written about those tired old clichés and about greed, ambition, bigotry, hypocrisy. It all depends on who writes them. Read Shakespeare, Tolstoy, the Old Testament. You remember me saying to you once that there was something in your peasant soul hurting to come out, but that you were too scared to let it out? Well, I'm am no peasant. I don't know what's

hurting inside of you. But let it out. Not as preachment,
you fool, but as entertainment."

From then on, Capra tried to express that deeper human spirit
in all of his films. Every one of his films had a dramatic moment
when the protagonist had hit bottom, had walked through the valley of death, was given a second chance, and was able to find that
deepest spirit which, because of that discovery, redeemed him/
herself in the climax of the film.

There is nothing corny about a Frank Capra film because there
is nothing corny about the redemption of the best spirit within
ourselves. And most modern directors, the hippest among them,
talk about doing a "Capra" film during their lives. They want to
reach that wondrous moment, that art has of being able to redeem
that sacred spirit that lives within our soul.

How can you let it in and have it be a part of your life?

First, remember it.

It has been there at important times. It may have been there on
a Christmas morning when you were very young and innocent.
You thought magically. You knew something wonderful was in the
air. You didn't know exactly what, but you felt the spirit.

Or on a birthday, you knew it was your special day. And that
it was important that you were born. And that spirit within you
celebrated with full jubilation.

Or when you fell in love. Or when you looked at a sunrise for
the first time. Or when you first tasted a chocolate chip cookie. Or
your first sweet kiss. Or in a dream that you couldn't quite remember, but the feeling of well-being surrounded you, fixed in time for
an hour or more.

Many people would say these are immature and sophomoric
experiences. As you get older, you need to grow up, which means
become jaded, sophisticated and cynical. *They'll take your soul if you
let them, but don't you let them…*

Just below the surface is that deeper spirit which is so an essential part of you that you instinctively recognize it, and you feel
elated when you know it's there. It is forever young, forever wise
and mature. It is forever the real you.

Choose to let it into your life

To do that, decide you want it in your life. Choose to let it have a voice. In the middle of an important meeting, let yourself see beyond the circumstances to the deeper reality of your life-spirit. When you are trying to hold things together, becoming more determined and serious, let yourself flash on the absurdity of the human condition, the Cosmic Joke, and the fact that no matter how things are at the current moment, there is a precious inner pot of gold that generates its own rainbow. Notice it when it is there in abundance. Reach for it when it is hidden from your view.

Take a deeper look into yourself

There are depths to you that can become a powerful source of your own spirit. These depths can be explored and developed. This subject is discussed more fully in the next chapter.

Then, be open to it, and let it express itself in your life

When you become open to your deeper spirit, when you choose to have it in your life, it will find ways to express itself. You don't have to manage it, simply let it have a place at the table, and it will be a good member of the party. And, while they'll take your soul if you let them, *don't you let them. No, No*.

C h a p t e r   4

A Look Deeper in

M any of the guests who appear on our TV series *Creating* say that there is something extraordinary they encounter, something that fuels their creative process. Many artists throughout history have told of something beyond the surface, something that seemed to be a different dimension that, once explored, was generative, that changed their art, that changed them, changed their understanding, and created meaning,insight, and awareness within them.

When you create your life as art, you, as artist, can take a look "deeper in," and this act can profoundly change you. But as we explore this step, we need to be careful...very careful indeed, because it is easy to slip into psychological delusion, philosophic rhetoric and spiritual conjecture which will work against our ability to look and see what there is to see.

There is a common flaw we suffer as human beings. Once we experience something that is beyond words, we then put words to it. Often the words do not do justice to the experience itself, but we begin to look to the words rather than to the original experience they are designed to reference.

When we explore the deeper territories of ourselves, we should never let the experiences be limited by the words we use to explain them. Even more importantly, we should not let the words *others* have used to describe their experiences bias our deeper look. Their words should not become our goals. Words about the type of experiences we are talking about can become petrified into a philosophy or worldview. The ideas coagulate into fixed ideals. What began as authentic exploration can drift into a search for confirmation of what we think. We can't say it's really a true exploration if we only look for experiences that confirm our hypothesis.

So, in writing this section, I am trying to point out a direction for your own authentic exploration, and not a simple "search and find" mission based on the reports of others, or even ideas you currently hold.

To look authentically within ourselves, we need to learn to look in a very special way. We need to adopt a very unusual orientation, that of looking *without reaching for anything, or searching for anything, or even expecting anything.*

If we were on a quest to find virtuous treasures such as enlightenment, inner peace, bliss, etc., etc., etc., we might fail to discover what there was to discover. Our agenda limits our exploration by giving us standards by which to measure our "success." If you're looking for an elephant, you might miss the mouse. And if you're looking for a mouse, you just might miss the elephant in front of you.

Begin Without an Agenda

Here's a helpful principle: For it to be *real*, we can't begin our look deeper in with an agenda, especially one that dictates what we are presumed to find. Beginning with goals rigs the search. What we have found may have been conjured up by trying to satisfy our assumptions.

And in our society there are many books, articles, workshops, teachers, authorities, gurus, experts, pop-mystics, and TV personalities who are ready, willing, and more than able to tell you what you should be seeing when you consider your deeper self.

It is easy for us to get an impression that we must learn and experience the answers others have reached. I don't doubt the experience or enthusiasm of the authors. But we need to avoid using their ideas as our marching orders. And this is one reason, that in this section, I will avoid telling you about my personal experiences when I look more deeply into myself. I want to encourage you to look, but not to try to see what I have seen.

Whatever we find must be seen *because it was there to see*, and not because we invented it based on ours or others preconceptions. If we're not trying to accomplish spiritual progress, or achieve psychological resolution, or have a mystical experience, or develop greater powers and abilities, or comprehend the ultimate answers to life, we have a good chance to explore the unknown territory of ourselves authentically. So look without a list of expected or desired outcomes.

Why look, if not to find all these wonderful benefits listed above? That's a good question.

And the good answer is *truth*…for truth's sake. We might call our journey the "*aimless pursuit of reality.*"

The Instinct to Look

There is an instinct in us to look more deeply into life. We want to know what's around the next hill, what's under the sea, what's in outer space, even what's in our friend's bathroom cabinets. Curiosity comes in many forms, and one of the most instinctive forms is that of seeing what's within us.

This instinct isn't satisfied by our beliefs. We can even say that belief can take us away from looking more deeply into ourselves because if you think you know something, you are less likely to explore, ask vital questions, delve more deeply, and probe.

Many beliefs give one the illusion of knowing something they simply do not know. But the illusion can be so self-convincing that reality seems to be unquestionably consistent with the belief. If something is unquestionable, why ask questions or explore other possibilities?

Moving Beyond Belief

To create the life you want, it doesn't matter what you believe. And, even more importantly, what you believe is irrelevant to looking more deeply into yourself. You may be an atheist, or a believer in God, or an agnostic. You can be a mystic or a materialist. You can believe in life after death or believe that death is final annihilation. You can believe that life has a purpose or not. That humanity is on the track of spiritual progress or that humanity is caught in a loop of repeated patterns as the generations pass. You can believe in religion or science or both or neither. You can believe in destiny or random chaos. The look deeper in doesn't require holding "the right beliefs."

It might be argued that your beliefs will determine what you do, but if we look more closely, we see that people have other more important drives, more important than simply their beliefs.

Some people believe in celibacy, but are not celibate. Some people believe in democracy, but do not vote regularly. Most of us are capable of firmly holding both a belief and it's opposite. Our beliefs are not always consistent with our behavior.

It's true that people fight with each other over their various beliefs. Some of the most vicious wars in history were religious and the major difference between one side and another was a variation of the same basic belief.

People fight over philosophy, aesthetics, the basic nature of humanity, if scientific research is beneficial or destructive, etc.

There are many contradictory beliefs for us to fight over if we want to. So, if we are to look more deeply into ourselves, we hope to discover something more substantial than belief.

Since it is critical to begin the exploration *without* a concept about what you might find, you must suspend what you believe. This is not to say you need to give up your beliefs, just that you shouldn't use them. Leave them at the door on your way in. You can pick them up on your way out, if you still want them.

What We Shouldn't Look For

For the search to be real, there are some things for which we shouldn't look.

• We shouldn't look for solutions to life's problems — although some of life's problems may clear up, or become unimportant even if they remain.

• We shouldn't search for our purpose in life — although we might find a sense of purpose as we look deeper into ourselves.

• We shouldn't look for salvation, although we might find ourselves saved.

Look, not for an answer, but to see what there is to see.

Looking More Deeply

How does one look more deeply?

You may meditate, soul search, think, ask yourself questions, observe, be open to what's truest in you, deepest in you, highest in you. The openness is not a drive toward a goal, but only an area of exploration that can be probed.

And don't just look once, but throughout your life, and often. Rethink everything. Rethink what you think you know, conclusions you've made, ideas you've come to, assumptions you've made, the meaning of experiences you've had. Rethink age-old questions: what is the meaning of life...or better yet, does life have a meaning?

Looking this way is a solo flight. There are many profound experiences people have when they are together, focused collectively. They may have a spiritual experience with group meditation or in formal religious services. They may feel the spirit in a Gospel concert or in a rock concert. They may sense the height of human experience while watching a great film in a theater, or while seeing a play. There is a type of collective experience that can be very moving and penetrating to the soul. And these experiences are truly great and important. But the look deeper in we are talking about is on a different level. Looking on your own is neither a substitute for a collective experience, nor is a collective experience a substitute for a solo exploration.

As you look deeper into yourself, one type of experience you can have is this: you come into the presence of this...thing. You may think of it from a religious point of view or a secular point of view or a metaphysical point of view. But however you try to describe it, it will lose something in the translation.

This thing, this energy, this spirit, this presence comes, not by seeking it, but rather by allowing it.

On the one hand, we make it possible to experience by being open to it, but the ironic quality of being open means being also open to this experience *not occurring*.

The aimless pursuit of reality is not driving toward a goal, save the goal of seeing what there is to see whatever it is. When we are able to look without an agenda, we observe, and this observation creates a wonderful fusion of active and passive. To observe is not passive. But to be open to see whatever there is to see is passive. This passive act creates a "vacuum", or empty space that can be filled by the observation.

If we are trying to fill it ourselves with our own concepts, we can't see. We will be projecting our beliefs on the screen, and it will no longer be possible for us to truly observe. We will not be able to be in the presence of anything except our own notions.

But, if we don't fill in the spaces, and we look, we will be able to be in the presence of what there is to see, feel, perceive, intuit, experience, and sense. Sometimes, this openness to looking results in finding. We can be filled. Some have described it as bathed. Others have called it anointed. Others have not called it anything, because whatever you say about it doesn't do it justice.

Is this a good experience to have? Yes, but don't make it your goal. Don't set a trap for it, don't try to trick it, don't glorify it, and don't celebrate it.

It's our nature to take something and put form around it. But when we do that, we sometimes take something away from the thing itself.

The looking without the need for an answer helps you see what there is to see, and sometimes for some people that means finding God. For others, it means finding nothing. For some it leads to inner strength and resolve, for others it leads to the deepest existential questions there are.

For some it leads to more and more questions, and for some it leads to the suspension of questions.

Whatever you find, you will be more in touch with what we might call the source of your life. We may not be able to say exactly what that is, but most people who work in the arts experience a source of their quest to create. Our human tendency is to define it. But, what I am trying to describe is somewhat beyond description.

For many of us, it is an experience of God. But it's important to understand that for many others it is not an experience of God. No one has to win, because what you find is what you find. There is no basis for an argument. If someone finds God, that doesn't invalidate someone's experience who finds something else. If someone finds something else, that doesn't invalidate the experience of one who finds God.

Finding God is not the goal of looking. But if you look without the agenda of finding God, and you find God, isn't it more accurate to say that God found you?

If you find that there is nothing to find, then what you've have found is that the source of life you rely on is from you, and you can be self-generating. The nothing can be a help in creating your life as art, and finding God can be a help in creating your life as art.

We must remember that every culture has art, and people from every belief system make art. The creation of art is philosophically neutral in that it doesn't matter what you believe to be able to create, any more than it does to drive a car, ski, play baseball, or eat food.

But, if what you might find is God or Christ or Buddha or Allah or white light or pure love or energy or universal mind or anything else, it is truly yours. It's not because you learned it from others who profess it, or because you thought it was a good idea. *It is yours and it becomes a true foundation and pillar in your life. It becomes your own personal spring from which to draw sustenance.*

From this deeper look, your life will change. It will become more real and vital, although these benefits are not the reasons to look. It's just that you will be in contact with another dimension that gives you more dimension.

Is it a source of energy? Yes. Is it power? Yes. But whatever this thing is, it is not something you manufacture. Rather it is something that you can be open to and can evoke, although evocation is perhaps too active a word to describe the actual relationship between what you can do and what it will do.

Here's an image to consider: There's something within you, which, as you look more deeply into yourself, you can sometimes find. And you find it by not looking for it but by observing whatever there is to see. And if you're open to seeing anything that's there, and if it's really there, it will appear.

Chapter 5

Frames of Reality

Years ago I saw a program on TV's *60 Minutes* which featured a psychiatrist who specialized in working with patients who had suffered losses in their lives, but couldn't recover. He spends one intense week with each of his patients. Throughout that week, the subject is reality.

The program showed him working with a woman who had lost her fifteen-year-old daughter years before. She had tried various forms of therapy and other approaches to bring her relief from her anguish, but nothing seemed to work. *60 Minutes* showed scenes of the doctor working with this poor grieving mother.

In one scene, the psychiatrist was siting at a table with the mother. He had several artifacts from the girl's life, and he was asking the mother to pick them up and say what they were. As she did this, her tears began to flow. At one point, he had her look at the daughter's picture. "Look at that face," he said. The mother was now crying. "What a beautiful face," the doctor went on. The mother's crying increased. "Yes what a beautiful face," she agreed. Then the doctor said, "And you'll never see her again."

Later in the program, doctor and patient were walking down a country lane. During the walk, he was explaining to the mother that her daughter had drowned years before. In various ways, the doctor was hitting the mother with a hard-to-accept reality. Sometimes he did it in quite shocking ways, sometimes in gentle ways. Over and over, he told her the truth about what had happened.

By the end of the week, a dramatic change had occurred for the mother. She began to understand that reality was what it was, even though it was exceedingly painful. She was not simply accepting reality at that point. She was embracing it, hard as that was. The past would not change, and her attempts to hold on to the past when her daughter was alive would not bring back her daughter.

The Truth Will Set You Free

When we are not able to live in current reality, we become trapped in the past. Usually this happens because we are rejecting reality. Rejecting it because we don't like it. We try to overcome the unacceptable events by ignoring them. As time moves on, our insistence that things weren't the way they actually were produces a wider and wider gap between then and now. When this happens, unless we can rejoin reality, we will be unable to create our lives.

This psychiatrist enabled the patient to become fluent in the reality she was trying to reject. A short period of only a week reviewing the events that had taken place profoundly change the patient. In a very real sense, she was reborn. In rejecting the reality of her daughter's death, she had rejected her own life. She couldn't go on with life while she was unwilling to face the awful truth. Once she faced it, she was, in a very real sense, healed.

60 Minutes went back a year later to see if the change had lasted. It had. She said that she would always miss her daughter, but from that week on, she was able to begin to live her life again.

There is a power to truth that is, indeed, freeing. The freedom is not always freedom from pain, hurt, sadness, grief, anguish, or agony. But it is the freedom to go forward and build your life, even though you may carry the scars of past losses with you.

When we engage in the creative process, we can begin with a blank sheet of paper, a clean white canvas, an empty stage, a fresh roll of film in the camera, and, as the record producer often says, "take 2," meaning that we can record another version of the music. No matter what the past has been and how ineffectively we have dealt with it, life has a way of always giving us another chance. It isn't always the same chance. It's usually a new and different type of chance to join reality and begin to create again.

Our ability to live in reality is essential. But this takes training. It may mean that you need to take a stand in favor of the truth.

Growing In Awareness

What do we mean by truth? Is truth simply an objective perception of reality?

Seeing reality objectively must be developed. In the long tradition of the arts, students learn to increase their level of awareness. In fact, that phrase "increase your level of awareness" was one that all of us as students heard repeatedly at the Boston Conservatory of Music. We had extensive courses in ear training in which we would listen to records. We were taught how to hear the orchestration, the harmony, the rhythm, the counterpoint, the inner voicing of the lines. We were tested on how well we could hear a recording by writing the music down. This was called a record copy, and our teachers would show us what they were after by listening to an orchestra or a big band arrangement, and writing it on the blackboard as fast as they could. Our teachers prided themselves on being tough. If we got one note wrong, our grade went down from an A to a B. If we got two notes wrong, we were graded C. Any more and we didn't pass. Our teachers explained it this way: If we were in a recording studio in professional circumstances, and we had to fix a note because we got it wrong, that would take time away from the session. In professional situations like that, time is not only money, it's a whole lot of money. The production costs would go up because of our mistake. So, they were teaching us that there were consequences to our actions, and that we needed to learn how to "raise our level of awareness."

Years later, I was teaching at Berklee College, where years earlier Quincy Jones was a student. People who had worked with Quincy as a student always talked about how perfect his scores were. Even as a young man, he had "raised his level of awareness" and was as perfect as anyone could be. Even before he had become a living legend in the world of music, he was a legend in Boston.

Art students go through rigorous basic training to help them better see reality. At first, they don't see it well, which limits their ability to draw and paint. Even the most talented of them need to learn to observe a scene as it truly is.

Kimon Nicolaides, in his classic book *The Natural Way to Draw*, said, "There is only one right way to learn to draw and that is a perfectly natural way. It has nothing to do with artifice or technique. It has nothing to do with aesthetics or conception. It has only to do with the act of correct observation, and by that I mean a physical contact with all sorts of objects through all the senses. If a student misses this step and does not practice it for at least his first five years, he has wasted most of his time and must necessarily go back and begin all over again."

Painter and teacher Arthur Stern said, "The mind stands in the way of the eye." And, "They [students] paint what they *expect* to see."

Art students need to learn to "see" reality, because in the beginning of their training they see only their *concepts* of reality.

We develop various pictures, ideas, and ideals about the world. And instead of carefully viewing reality, we impose these ideas on our perceptions. As Sherlock Holmes always said to poor old Watson, "You see, but you do not observe." We may all be Watson at first. But we need to become Holmes. We need to see *and* observe.

If we are to create our life as art, we need to improve our "eye." That is to say, we need to better understand what is truly going on in reality, so that the mind is *not* standing in the way of the eye, as Stern so aptly described. We need to shift away from our concepts, beliefs, ideals, past experiences and theories influencing our perception of reality, to our conscious observations enabling us to reach more objective understanding.

Reality and Structural Tension

Without a good fix on reality, we can't establish structural tension, the dynamic that is needed for us to create our goals.

If we frame reality well, we have better tension on our bow with which to aim our arrow. If we have not framed reality well, our bow is limp and we will not be able to generate adequate tension to reach the target.

On the level of mechanics, framing reality properly is essential. With the right frame, we will know how to organize our current actions and how to adjust future actions.

Violinists play in tune because they listen as they play. They will make ongoing adjustments to their pitch to stay in tune with themselves and the rest of the orchestra. They use a feedback system in which they aim for a note, they listen to the note they have produced, and they refine their pitch as needed.

If we were violinists who were tone deaf, we would have a lot of trouble playing in tune because we could not discern the relationship between what we were playing and what everyone else in the orchestra was playing. Not hearing pitch dooms us to an inability to adjust our pitch when we need to. In a similar way, the inability to be fluent in reality will limit our capacity to learn from our actions, adjust them as needed, and get a fix on where we are in relationship to our goals.

From an orientational point of view, how we deal with reality reflects our values and the personal issues we may have. For most people, reality is an acquired taste. Reality is not always pleasant, nor convenient, or comforting.

How much do we want to know the truth as it actually is, especially when it is in conflict with how we would like things to be? Many people have a conflict between their desire to know reality and their desire to minimize conflict and strife.

We have moments of truth in life. Truth blatantly stares us in the face. These are moments that define our values. If we embrace the truth, even though it is hard or inconvenient, we have defined ourselves by our expressed value that truth is more important to us than avoiding conflict. We may see that we have been wrong in dealing with a loved one. We have a choice. We can admit it and apologize, or ignore the truth, hoping to avoid the internal conflict we might feel if we acknowledge our mistake. We may know that our teenagers are staying out too late. Even though we know there will be a parent-teenager showdown, full of discord and strife, we might sit him down and talk about it anyway. On the other hand, to avoid an ugly confrontation, we might pretend we don't notice the time he comes home.

If we turn away from the truth at this moment, we are expressing a different value: We will distort reality when it suits us. Many people have been brainwashed into thinking that they are too emotionally frail to face truth directly. The fact is we can take the truth. We have the capacity, stamina, and inner strength to see the truth exactly as it is. And when we *choose* to, we gain a new possibility in life. Truth often precedes transcendence, the chance we are sometimes given in life to begin afresh.

The Discipline of Reality

We have an itch and, we scratch — that is natural. We have an itch, and we don't scratch — that's a discipline.

It is natural for us to avoid pain and conflict. So, seeking the truth is not something we do by nature. It is a discipline, and like every discipline, is *not* natural. As we build our life as art, one discipline we will need to master is fluency in reality. We need to know exactly how it is. We will need to raise our level of objectivity, discernment, and awareness.

On the level of spirit, reality is all we ever have in the current moment, and our relationship to it will either expand or limit our life-expression. Many Eastern disciplines such as Yoga and Zen focus their students on a greater understanding and perception of the current moment. In the West, the arts are filled with similar disciplines. One of the great developments in acting technique is the ability for the actor to be fully present to reality. When Dennis Hopper and James Dean were working on the film *Giant*, Hopper asked Dean to watch him act and give him pointers. After playing a scene, Dean asked Hopper what he was doing. "I was concentrating on my acting," Hopper said. "What do you do with the crew (camera personnel, lighting people, sound team, etc.)," Dean asked. "I ignore them," Hopper answered. "That's you're mistake." Dean said, "Pay attention to them. Pay attention to everything that is going on, and use it in your performance."

Our ability to focus our attention can be developed, expanded, and fine-tuned. There are many wonderful techniques that are available. A simple Yoga technique is a meditation in which we sit quietly, close our eyes and then "watch" our breathing. Our focus is directed to that one natural activity. After several minutes, our minds begin to become sharper and more relaxed. This technique helps to increase our level of awareness in the moment.

Another technique I like is a simple focusing technique. We sit comfortably in a straight-back chair. We close our eyes, take a few deep breaths, and relax. We then begin to focus on one of our hands. All we do is pay attention to that hand. If other thoughts begin to enter our minds, we gently shift our attention back to our hand. After a few minutes, we will begin to feel energy in that hand. After a few minutes we begin to move the focus around. We shift the focus to the top of our heads. We hold that focus for a

short time. And then we shift to other parts of the body: the fore-
head, the throat, the chest, the stomach, the legs, the arms, etc.
After shifting our focus, we concentrate on the hand again, and
hold that focus for a minute or two. And then we take another
deep breath, relax our focus, and in another moment or two, we
open our eyes.

Techniques like these are very beneficial in many ways. They
help the mind relax. They help us sharpen our focus. They help us
stay in the current moment of reality. And they increase our level
of awareness.

Framing Reality

One of the challenges we have when we begin to use structural tension is that we may have to think differently. We may
have to change from thinking linearly in small units to thinking
dimensionally in larger units. How can we make this shift?

Imagine we had our good old video camera again. Using this
metaphor, we could shoot a *close-up*, a *medium shot*, or a *long shot*
of reality.

We have a habit of looking at the world through one of these
camera positions. We can change our position in the same way
that we can with the dynamic urge. There, we can move our focus
from appetites, impulses, vague hopes, and longings to aspirations
and values. In a similar way, we may need to reposition the lens
with which we view the world.

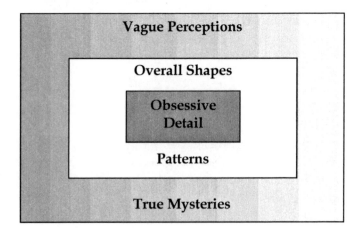

The Close Up:
Immediate Events and Obsessive Detail

Some people use the close-up as their primary frame of reference, focusing on the immediate events that confront them. They tend to obsess about details but can often miss what the various details, put together, imply.

The world is filled with people who use immediate events and obsessive detail as their frame of reference. We can see this idiosyncrasy by how they relate to time. Time, to these people, comes in short phases. Their focus is on details and small bits of information. They can become overwhelmed quite easily, for there is always more information in life than we can deal with.

These people see the world as very complicated and hard to manage. They often have high aspirations and deeply held values, but their way of relating to reality greatly limits their effectiveness. In spite of their aspirations, they often feel forced to react or respond to their immediate circumstances. They often feel like they are treading water.

But even if you have had your lens zoomed in on a close-up your entire life, the good news is that you can zoom back. You can change your frame to one that is much more useful and effective.

The Long Shot: Chronic Vagueness

If we zoom back too far, we can no longer make out what we are seeing. Some people look at the world through a lens that is so wide that everything seems to fuse together in a jumbled haze. They know that something is there, but they can't quite make out what it is. These people think in very long time periods, and they often ponder the distant future more than the current reality.

People who live in the long shot quite often speculate about how the world is. They have many theories. This is because, without a clear view of current reality, it gives them a way to get their bearings.

If we are in an extreme long shot, we can change our lens to a medium shot. We can then shift from the haze of vagueness to the clarity of seeing overall shapes and patterns in reality.

The Medium Shot:
Objective Shapes, Trends, and Patterns

The medium shot enables us to observe both the forest and the trees. We can make out details, but we can also recognize the relationships these details form. As we back away from a close up, or move in from a long shot, we reach a point where we can view overall shapes and reoccurring patterns.

Within a medium shot, our time frame is different than it is from the other two frames. As we observe the present, we also see how the present connects with the past. We also see how the present may lead to the future.

If a baseball player hit a ball toward center field, and the ball was high in the air and moving out fast, we would be able to predict to some degree where it is likely to land. This is why sports announcers can watch a solidly hit baseball sail out toward the fence and say "Going! Going! Gone!" If they couldn't predict where the ball might land, they would have to say "Don't know, don't know...oh, wow, it suddenly went over the wall!"

Both the close-up and the long shot give us information, but they are like non-relational databases; the information cannot connect with other information.

But the medium shot is like a relational database in which things that do in fact connect can be *seen* as connecting.

Structural Tension: The Best Frames

The very best way to frame structural tension is to have two medium shots: one for the dynamic urge and one for current reality.

This arrangement will give us the most tension on our bow with which to aim our arrow.

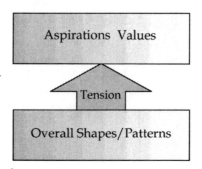

Part of our job is to learn how to frame our desires. Part of our job is to frame current reality in relationship to our goals. As we establish structural tension on this level, we are using the most powerful structural dynamic there is. We are stacking the deck in our favor. We are increasing our chances of creating the results we want. We are setting up a path that can lead us to the life we want to create.

Structural tension generates actions. It helps us organize them strategically, and it helps motivate us to act effectively. Without structural tension, the actions you take are forced. It can feel like you are overcoming obstacles. You may engage in self-manipulation. This will only work for a short time at best. Soon, it will be hard to sustain your action plan.

Action: The Road to Your Goals

One thing that we hear over and over from the sports medicine community is that walking is good exercise, and if we take regular walks we can gain enormous health benefits. Every New Year's, when people make their resolutions, walking is often on the list.

But then we get busy. Much too busy. And this very simple thing becomes harder and harder. And when we think about it, we begin to feel guilty, and then we decide not to think about it...and we don't, until the year turns one more time.

(While I'm addressing these remarks to those of you who *don't* walk, for those of you who *do*, pick your own suitable example.)

Now, I'm not telling you to take a walk, although that's maybe what you should do for your own health and well being. I'm more using this example of human nature to make two vital points that can help you better create your life.

Easy and Hard

For most of us, it's easy to take a walk. That is to say, it's easy to actually walk, it's easy to take a small part out of our day and do it, and it's easy to schedule it into our lives so that it becomes an activity that builds over time.

So, if it's easy, why is it so hard to pull off? And here's one of the points: It's hard because it's easy. I know, you're thinking, let me have that again. Okay, here it is again...

It's hard because it's easy!

When things are very easy to do, we often think they have limited value. This impression is simply an absurd bias that many of us have picked up in our lives. We think that if it is too easy, it isn't worth it.

If you're the proud owner of this bias, you don't need to figure out how you came to own it. You need only to see that in reality *it's not true*.

Again, using walking as an example...

If it's so good for us and it's easy to do, and it doesn't take a lot of time, and it may extend our lives, then why don't we do it more often?

Here's the pattern we often find. See if it fits.

We decide to walk, and on the first day out, we walk and walk and walk. We exhaust ourselves, and because of that experience, we don't want to repeat it. We make what can be easy, harder than it has to be.

Here's a question for you. Do you have a pattern of making things harder in your life than they have to be? If you do, you're not alone. Lot's of us do that. And, before you feel better, (because misery loves company,) let's admit that it's a bad pattern and not one you want.

The pattern follows these steps:

- Make it harder than it has to be, *followed by*
- Losing interest in doing it, *followed by*
- Convincing yourself that it doesn't need doing.

The last step in this pattern can sound like this: "I don't need to formally go on walks. I walk a lot during the day anyway. It's as if I'm going on walks, so what's the difference?" Sorry, it's different. If you want more information about how it's different, ask your doctor.

But we're not talking about walking exactly. No, we're talking about a pattern and illustrating it with this example. There are many things you could be doing for yourself that would be easy to do, but you don't do them. If you did do them, you would see a change for the better, but still you don't do them. Why?

As you think about this question, forget giving yourself a pep talk, or trying to guilt trip yourself into better behavior. Notice that it didn't work the last three thousand times you tried that, at least not for long and not permanently. But you are not stuck with the pattern either. You just need some knowledge and then some experience about how to make things that could work for you…well, *work* for you.

On the road to creating a new and better pattern, our first step is this insight: Easy is often good. The value of an action cannot and should not be measured by the magnitude of its difficulty, *but by its impact on the result you are trying to create.*

Step two is an insight about motivation and truth.

> Fact: Most people who *don't* exercise, don't exercise because *they don't like to exercise.*

You might want to read that last sentence again.

The truth is that there are things that are good for you that you don't like doing. And if you did like doing them, you'd do them. You would be automatically motivated to do them. You don't need to convince yourself to eat a wonderful meal, or enjoy good company, or laugh at a funny joke. You can easily do so, as the old song says, "by doing what comes naturally."

Here's an image to consider for a moment:

It's easy but you don't like doing it.

What are the chances you will do "it" (whatever the "it" is)? Low. Very low, especially if it takes doing "it" for extended periods of time.

So, here's something for us to know about ourselves:

We don't like doing things we don't like doing.

And once we understand this little truth, we can stop trying to pretend we do like what we don't like in order to motivate ourselves. We are never in a good position with ourselves when we lie. We've been taught to lie, to think that somehow we do, should, or can like what we don't like. But we can't.

Nevertheless, sometimes things we don't like are actually good for us. Even more importantly, they serve to support things we very much want. While we may not want to take a walk every day, we do want to support our own health and well-being.

We now get to the insight about motivation: *If there is an important enough reason to do something, we will probably do it.*

The Bankruptcy of Carrots and Sticks

We are often given good arguments by well meaning people about why we should take this or that action. For example: "Floss your teeth or you will lose them." And if you don't want to be toothless, it's not a bad argument. But, just because it's a good argument, doesn't mean we will floss our teeth, at least, not for long. Yes, we might do it for a few days or a week, but the fear of a life of toothlessness soon fades from our minds, and we are skipping flossing, first one or two times a week, and then more, and then more, and then it's no longer a regular practice.

This type of argument—do "it" or suffer the negative consequences—is a form of conflict manipulation. Conflict manipulation is one of the most common ploys in our society to get us to behave better. Here's how it works: we are given an image of terrible catastrophes, enough to instill fear, concern, anxiety, and consternation in us. We are then filled with apprehension, and we want the uncomfortable emotion to stop. We react against the feelings we are having, and we take action. But the action we take is motivated by wanting the bad feelings to go away. So we floss, or eat less red meat, or exercise, or quit smoking. We take the action that is recommended to prevent the awful thing from happening.

And we begin to feel better. Now, if you think that feeling better encourages us to continue this beneficial action, think again. Instead of continuing, at this point we falter, and then revert back to our old ways. Why?

Remember *why* we did what we did? We felt badly, and we wanted to rid ourselves of such terrible feelings. When we took some action, we began to feel better about it all. The intensity of the bad feelings drove us into action, which reduces the intensity of the bad feelings. Less bad feelings, less motivation to act. Less motivation to act, less the tendency for us to act. And sure enough, we are not able to sustain the positive behavior we began.

Most people at this point are convinced they have a grave character flaw, and that's why they can't maintain good practices. They may try the old guilt trip on themselves. And this may begin a new, short-lived, episode of conflict manipulation. They feel so badly about what weak-willed wimps they are, that they take action to feel better about themselves. They go through a new round of flossing, or eating less red meat, or exercising, or quitting smoking. Then they feel better about themselves. The motivation that drove the new behavior is reduced, and sooner or later, they are back to their old habits.

Robert Frost said, " I never tried to worry anybody into intelligence."

A Carrot Anyone?

If fear of negative consequences is not a good motivation for taking effective action, what's the alternative? One alternative that is often adopted, but is equally weak, is the carrot in the famous carrot and stick analogy. The carrot comes in the form of all the good benefits that will happen if we take the action. In this approach, images of success flood our minds, and we are given all the positive reasons why we should do what we would rather not do. The argument is we should do it for the rewards. The rewards are often put in terms of enhanced self-image, feelings of satisfaction, or perhaps even rewards in heaven. The thought is that if we keep a positive outlook, and affirm positive statements, we will be able to program our subconscious mind, which in turn will produce success for us. This tact is called *will-power manipulation*. Usually through a series of pep talks, positive motivational tapes, self-propaganda, and declarations of faith in ourselves, we are "inspired" to act.

The always useful question: What do you do on days you are not inspired? And if you survey your life, you find more uninspired days then inspired. And to try to stay inspired is the other side of the coin of staying in conflict.

Neither fear nor inspiration can last for long, because these experiences are in constant flux. Think of them as the weather. They are what's going on in the atmosphere, but, like the weather, the condition will change. Just as fear driven action will reduce the fear, inspiration driven action will reduce the inspiration, especially as we get into the nuts and bolts of the action process. A "positive" argument is as weak as a "negative" argument, and we need something more substantial than action that runs off our emotions, good, bad, or indifferent.

We need a real reason to act. And by reason I mean motivation, not just an argument.

Choosing What's Really Important To Us

Why would we do something that we don't like doing in and of itself? Because of what the action supports. This point gives us the key to true discipline.

Let's think about the *relationship* between actions we don't particularly like, and outcomes we want to achieve. What is the relationship? *It is secondary to primary.* Primary means *first* and therefore everything else is less important.

If I want to learn to play the piano, I need to spend time practicing. I may not want to practice, for, after all, I'm practicing things I'm not very good at. I must suffer through my own mistakes, my own inabilities, my own frustrations, and boredom. While I may want to be a pianist, I don't particularly want to be a piano student.

In reality, there are *two* things I want. One is to be a competent pianist, and the other is to spend my time in more enjoyable ways than the frustration of practice time. But, these two things are mutually exclusive in that I can't have one without giving up the other. Here are all my choices, and they are limited:

> • Give up my attempt to be an accomplished pianist so as to spend more enjoyable time (and less frustrating time);
>
> **or**
>
> • Put up with the frustrating experiences while learning to play the piano.

Some of you are thinking, "Hey, wait a minute, what about learning to like practicing."

That won't work. Sorry. Now, as you get better and better, you might begin to like practicing more than you did before, but that's not because you learned to like practicing, but because you are moving closer to your goal. The frustration level might be reduced, but there's a good chance you've not really learned to like practicing, but that you realize that it takes practice to succeed, and you are no longer making a big deal about it.

Please don't waste your time trying to like what you don't like. Instead, make strategic choices about what's more important to you, and what's less important to you. And I do mean *choice*.

What is a real choice? It means you can do it or not do it. I can play the piano or not. I can practice or not. But, there is a relationship in that one is inextricably tied to the other. The choice we can make in this example has to do with what's more important to us. If knowing how to play the piano is *MORE* important (primary) we can make a choice to support that outcome by doing something we don't like doing, namely, practicing (secondary.) In this case playing is more important than the discomfort of practice. We don't need to pretend we like practicing when we don't. We can tell ourselves the truth, which is we don't like it, but we will do what we don't like because we are motivated by a higher interest, the outcome we want to create.

Now, if it turned out that we want to spend more enjoyable time elsewhere than playing the piano well, the primary objective is our ease or comfort, and playing is less important. Therefore, in support of our higher objective, quitting study is a secondary choice we would make to further the cause.

We must learn to think *hierarchically*. We need to learn how to think in terms of what's more important to us, and what's less important to us, because if we don't, we might spend our whole lives consumed by actions, pursuits, activities, and events that matter very little to us. And it would be a shame for us to drift into such a life simply because we didn't know any better.

If we are clear about our motivation, we can more easily support our hierarchy. If we know that we want to play the piano, and it takes practice to pull it off, then we are ready to do something we otherwise wouldn't do. We are ready to spend time exposing ourselves to frustrating experiences, because it comes with the territory. We support our primary choice by making the necessary, strategic secondary choices.

So, if we didn't like to take regular walks, why might we do it, and more than that, why might we be motivated to do it? Because we very much do like the result it supports.

Over time, as we support those things that matter more to us by taking the necessary secondary choices it takes to succeed, we begin to experience a shift in orientation. We begin to develop a greater tolerance for doing things that we may not like on their own terms, because doing them supports a greater good. And sometimes, we become converts, in the sense that we may begin to actually like doing the thing we didn't like at first.

One word of warning! We may begin to like to walk, and that's fine. But we must not lose touch with the actual reason we are doing it. The danger is that if we begin to enjoy it, we may shift our standard of measurement from the health goal it supports, to the experience itself. This is not such a good transition because there may be days in the future in which we don't like to walk. If we've based the action on the enjoyment of the walk, then we can give up on the days we no longer enjoy it. Stay clear about your motives, and you will make consistent secondary choices, and your chances of success will go up and up.

So take a walk. And later, take a hike, if that better supports the goal of health. And be in touch with your primary choices so that you never slip into confusion as you go.

Moving into Action

Action within the context of structural tension is well motivated. Throughout the next three chapters, we will meet structural tension in various forms. The first look will be a simple application of it developed over a short time frame. The next examination of it will be from a very long-term vantage point. The view after that is a one-to-five year horizon. Each look is a different exploration at the same structural principle. Each one adds to our understanding of the next.

Short Term Creating

Let's practice structural tension and the principle of primary and secondary choice. Pick a result you want to create. For now, make it something small. Something you can create within the next few weeks or so. Something that is within your current abilities, capacity, talents. Something that you can fit into your busy schedule.

Got it? (If not, make one up.) Good.

Now get out a piece of paper. On the top of the paper, make a box.

Let's say that our goal is to have a Fourth of July lawn party. Our vision includes lots of different kinds of people from many different walks of life. We want to have about 30 or so people drop over during the day. We envision food being cooked on the barbecue, people swimming in the pool, kids playing games, people meeting each other and having a good time hanging out.

We also want to have a lot of fun ourselves. We want to set up the party so that everyone pitches in to help. The guests will bring some potluck dishes, and we'll provide the hot dogs, hamburgers, corn, watermelon, cold beer, and wine. We want perfect weather, but we may not be able to do much about that. We want people having one of the best times they have ever had at a Fourth of July lawn party.

Here's what Rosalind and I wrote for our party:

> A Fourth of July lawn party for about 30 or so interesting and diverse people. Great food, fun, swimming, hanging out, fun for the kids, good connections made as guests meet each other, guests join in and help, great weather, and people having one of the best times they have ever had at a Fourth lawn party.

This description isn't perfect. We imagine more than what we've written. But when we read this description, we know what we are after. We actually have a picture of the party. We can imagine the experience of being there. In our minds, we can imagine this wonderful event taking place on the Fourth of July, and we were all very glad we were there.

What you write in the top box does not need to be overly word-smithed. The first and most important idea is that you know what you mean. In a way, the words are simply a reminder.

On the other hand, the words do define some of the major parameters you want. Those things that can be quantified should be given numbers. Thirty or so guests give us a more actuate picture of how big the party is. Had we said, "lots of people," we wouldn't have been able to form the same picture. A little common sense makes sense when describing the outcome you are after.

A party isn't the most noble of causes. And that's why I choose it as an example. In this exercise, I am recommending small and rather insignificant goals. Such goals make a better experiment with which to practice. And while we know this little event will not change the world, isn't it great to be able to have a nice party once and a while?

Our idea for the party is more about people we like getting together to have fun than anything else. Everything else will be designed around this result. When you form your goals, it's important to know the essence of what you are after, no matter how you may have described it in words.

Even the idea of the guests joining in, rather than being waited on, is part of the spirit we want. In this party, people will help *make* the party, both by being there *and* by joining the work crew. This is a practical idea in that it makes it easier to manage logistics. But if we had a large staff to take care of everyone, the spirit would be quite different from the one we want in which everyone rolls up his or her sleeves.

What's Our Current Reality

Now that we've described our goal, at the bottom of the page, draw another box:

You will write a description of your current reality in this lower box.

Here's what Rosalind and I wrote:

> We have made out our guest list. We haven't invited anyone yet. We've created a nice e-mail animated invitation to send to people. We have some people's phone numbers, but not everyone. We've got enough plates, napkins, etc. We don't have Fourth of July decorations or table clothes. We don't have the wine and beer we need. The people we plan on inviting know how to get to our house. Most of them often bring pot luck dishes to parties. We have a number of pool toys for the kids. We don't have enough wine glasses. The garden looks great, but the lawn is growing very fast.

These two boxes help us form structural tension. We notice the contrast between the desired state and the actual state. This is a tension that generates actions so we can resolve the tension in favor of the accomplishment of our goal.

Creating Action Steps

Our next step is to list the actions. Our primary choice is having a great party. The actions we will take are our secondary choices. Some of those steps might be enjoyable, and some will not be as much fun. But all of them will be necessary to accomplish our goal.

We write them in-between the upper and lower boxes. At first, we will just list actions in any old order, and not think about their sequence. Later, once we list all the steps, we will put them in order. This makes it very easy for us to think about the various things we must do before, during, and after the party.

When we read the result and compare it to the current reality, we can see that many of the steps we need to take will be obvious.

> A Fourth of July lawn party for about 30 or so interesting and diverse people. Great food, fun, swimming, hanging out, fun for the kids, good connections made as guests meet each other, guests join in and help, great weather, and people having one of the best times they have ever had at a Fourth lawn party.

- Get phone numbers
- Call people on the list
- Rent wine and beer glasses
- Make a list of dishes people might want to bring
- Mow the lawn
- Send out e-mails
- Buy bug spray
- Arrange trash barrels around the lawn
- Buy Fourth of July decorations
- Update the pool maintenance

> We have made out our guest list. We haven't invited anyone yet. We've created a nice e-mail animated invitation to send to people. We have some people's phone numbers, but not everyone. We've got enough plates, napkins, etc. We don't have Fourth of July decorations or table clothes. We don't have the wine and beer we need. The people we plan on inviting know how to get to our house. Most of them often bring pot luck dishes to parties. We have a number of pool toys for the kids. We don't have enough wine glasses. The garden looks great, but the lawn is growing very fast.

These action steps are pretty easy to take. Yet, writing them down helps us see what we need to do to create the party. We get an overview from viewing the list of steps.

Now that we've done that, we are going to write a due date for each step. This puts the actions in the right order.

We will then rewrite the chart we are making, so that the earlier steps are on the bottom and the later steps are on the top. The steps remind us of a ladder, and as we climb up, we get closer to our goal.

Given that there are two of us arranging the actions, we may assign each step to one of us so that there's no confusion about who is doing what. R is for Robert and Rz is for Rosalind.

> *A Fourth of July lawn party for about 30 or so interesting and diverse people. Great food, fun, swimming, hanging out, fun for the kids, good connections made as guests meet each other, guests join in and help, great weather, and people having one of the best times they have ever had at a Fourth lawn party.*

- Mow the lawn—July 3rd *R*
- Shop for food and beverages—July 3rd *R*
- Arrange trash barrels around the lawn—July 3rd *R*
- Update the pool maintenance—July 2nd *Rz*
- Buy Fourth of July decorations—June 28th *Rz*
- Buy bug spray—June 28th *Rz*
- List dishes people might want to bring—June 25th *R*
- Rent wine and beer glasses—June 15th *Rz*
- Call people on the list—By June 9th *Rz*
- Send out e-mails—June 8th *R*
- Get phone numbers—June 6th *R*

> *We have made out our guest list. We haven't invited anyone yet. We've created a nice e-mail animated invitation to send to people. We have some people's phone numbers, but not everyone. We've got enough plates, napkins, etc. We don't have Fourth of July decorations or table clothes. We don't have the wine and beer we need. The people we plan on inviting know how to get to our house. Most of them often bring pot luck dishes to parties. We have a number of pool toys for the kids. We don't have enough wine glasses. The garden looks great, but the lawn is growing very fast.*

Even though this is a small project, it is helpful to have it organized so well. It took about six minutes to work it all out. Doing so saved us time and stress and made itall as easy as it could be.

So now, write in the action steps that you need to take to accomplish your goal. Remember to first write the various steps that will enable you to reach the result you want and then date them, putting them in a sequence. If there is more than one person taking the steps, it might be helpful to assign each step to one person. This will create greater clarity.

Remember that each action step is actually a secondary choice made within the context of a primary choice. You may like taking these actions or not, but their function is to support the outcome you are creating. That is the only standard of measurement that is critical to the process.

Create your goal. This type of exercise of creating small goals over a short period is like the sketches artists makes to develop technique. Of course, these goals have a place in our lives. But, more importantly, they are the practice sessions that help us better understand and master our own creative process.

Once you have conducted a first experiment with structural tension, and especially, structural tension *charting*, begin to design charts for more involved projects. Little by little, develop your skills. Not only are you learning the mechanics of the process, you will begin to assimilate structural tension more deeply into your consciousness.

The most powerful dynamic in your creative process is structural tension. We have visited it in this chapter by using it in small "practice" projects. The advantage in such projects is that we can experience the entire creative process from inception to completion in a short time frame. If we had begun to practice the creative process with goals that took a long time to complete, we would have had very little experience with the later stages of the process. It would have taken too long to reach the conclusion for it to be a good learning strategy. With shorter projects, we are learning how the parts of the cycle fit together as a whole as we create one result after another.

Creating Your Life
Long-Term

Now that we have explored the shorter time frames in using structural tension, it is time to think in longer time frames. How shall we consider what we want long-term?

Some principles that help us connect with our true desires and aspirations are useful at this point in our journey. These principles are intended to be evocative of your own inner truth and wisdom, but not set rules one must follow. Some of the principles are about the mechanics of your personal creative process. Some are important points about orientation. Understanding these principles can make all the difference between organizing your life around what you truly want, and organizing your life around distorted concepts of what you should want. Some principles will be directed toward the deeper spirit of your creative process and how you can touch the penetrating source of your own soul and spirit as it can manifest itself in your life.

Principle 1:

*Think about what you want to create rather
than what you want to eliminate*

Creating is about giving birth to something. Try out this thought experiment. In just a moment, when we begin this experiment, close your eyes. Once your eyes are closed, imagine yourself as a kind of center of expression, a source, a creator. In a moment after that, imagine energy beginning to flow, expand, and surge from you and through you. Further imagine that this energy is giving birth to something. In our imagination it doesn't matter what this something is yet. It may be just some shapeless, formless object. The point of the thought experiment is *feeling the gesture of giving birth to an idea,* and not as a focus on what you might create.

Now that you know what the process is, take a moment and try it out. It should only take from thirty seconds to a minute.

(Okay, go.)

That little experiment gives us a sense of what creating is about. We are bringing forth, directing and channeling energy, creating form and structure, focusing, and generating. Some of the most important insights about this technique come from what we are NOT doing. We are not problem solving, worrying, reacting to the circumstances, responding to the situation, avoiding anything, eliminating anything, fighting against anything, overcoming obstacles, or trying to defeat anything.

In creating your life as art, you are giving birth to the life you want, not getting rid of the life you don't want. If you create the life the way you want it to be, the unwanted things in your life may disappear, but often, that is because you have built something more powerful that takes the place of your old life.

There are times in the act of creating when you clear the decks, throw out superfluous clutter, eliminate distractions, simplify complexity, and so on. But the motivation for such activities is to support the creative process and is always linked to the final outcomes you are creating. The *motivation* for creating is bringing your creations into being, not solving problems or ridding yourself of unwanted circumstances.

Problem Solving Vs Creating

Many people pride themselves on being problem solvers. But a problem solving orientation limits your creative process. Let's consider what we are doing when we are problem solving.

First, our motivation is to rid ourselves of something we don't want rather than bring into being something we do want. This is the exact opposite of the motivation for creating.

Second, the problem *itself* is the factor that organizes our actions, not our desired outcomes.

Third, if we succeed in eliminating what we don't want, there is no guarantee that we will have what we do want.

Fourth, problem solving can lead to mindlessness, because our thoughts do not delve into issues of what we want, where we are in relationship to our goals, and how best to accomplish our desired results.

If you are a chronic problem solver, it's time to break the habit. While we can take a certain pride in our ability to solve problems, our orientation is so limited that it's best to shift to a more productive orientation. In a generative or creative orientation, our focus is on the outcomes we want to produce, not the unwanted circumstances we want to eliminate.

Problem solving has its place in our lives. But that place should be an exception to the norm.

Your Mind Doing Its Job

If your life consists of a lot of little problems or perhaps many very big problems, you may find you can only think in terms of problems. Your mind will automatically be "working" the problem because it wants resolution to the tension that it experiences. When you find yourself worrying and agonizing over a problematic situation, your mind is just doing its job. The mind is attempting to put order into disorder, explain discrepancies, unravel mysteries, untangle enigmas, and resolve tension. But you need to take control. If you don't, you can be overwhelmed during particularly difficult times in your life. You will experience progressive powerlessness because you can't solve the problems or immediately change the conditions you are in.

If your mind did not have the dynamic it does, it would realize that in such situations you are unable to take useful action. That realization would lead it to suspend its worry. Your mind would stop "working the problem." In an example of the type of cold logic that is atypical of the mind, Sherlock Holmes, in one of his mysteries, astonishes Watson yet again. In this particular story, Holmes comes to a point in which there is nothing he can do for the moment. Holmes suspends thinking about the mystery, and attends a concert, free of concern, the case temporarily put on hold. Our mind, undisciplined, would not be able to suspend itself when logic dictates it should. It would fret, worry, ponder, dread, brood and struggle. There is a very different operating principle involved with the mind, and it is consistent with the nature of structure. It wants to end discrepancies, resolve conflict, and above all else, establish equilibrium.

Your mind is going to be working on something or other. That's its nature. How can you use this characteristic of your mind productively? Here's one of the most effective ways: Give *your mind a bigger, more productive tension to work on*. If you don't, naturally it will gravitate toward the problems because it is trying to resolve the conflict the problems provoke.

The bigger tension to give your mind is *structural* tension. Let your mind focus on questions of how *it* will resolve the difference between the goals you envision and your current reality. Instead of letting your life be dominated by problems, begin to focus your attention, energy, creativity, and spirit on creating. Shift the topic from what you want to avoid, eradicate, or eliminate, to what you want to create, build, and produce. And let your mind help you in the process.

Principle 2:

Think about what you want to create rather than what it says about YOU

You are not what you create. And what you create is not a reflection of you. You are separate from what you create. You existed before you created it. It may exist after you no longer exist. You and your creation are two very different elements. In thinking about your life as art, you are not the artful life you create. It is a stage for the expression of the play you write. Your life is a vessel in which you travel. You are not the vehicle; you are the passenger, the captain, and the ship's designer.

In workshops, to provoke a full exploration of the true relationship between what the person does and who the person is, we ask people these questions: *Are you a better person if you are success-ful? Not as good a person if you are not?*

Many people begin this exploration with the notion that they would be a better person if they were more effective, successful, and productive. Perhaps you have this impression too.

Let's transform the question. We change the topic from success to driving. Are you a better person if you drive a car? Not as good if you don't drive? Suddenly, we can see that driving or not driving a car has nothing to do with the kind of person you are. If you went from a person who didn't know how to drive to a person who did, there would be no difference in your real value as a human being.

Let's change the topic to cooking. Are you a better person if you cook? Not as good if you don't?

Are you a better person if you know how to swim, not as good if you don't? Are you a better person if your belly button goes in? Goes out? It can get rather silly rather fast.

We have grown up in a culture in which success is linked with identity, as is failure. We are told that we are better, more useful, more valuable, more loveable, worthier of respect if we are successful. We can get the impression that our sense of self-worth and identity is tied to our degree of accomplishment. This is simply not true.

We are *not* what we do. We are whoever we are, and we do what we do. As creators, we are separate from our creation.

The more the creation takes on the role of representing you, the less freedom you have to fail. Why do you need freedom to fail? How else might you learn?

At the beginning of learning anything, even when we have natural talent, we will make plenty of mistakes. We will try to accomplish goals, benchmarks, tasks, and objectives, and many times we will fail at first. We fail because our ambition is greater at that point in our learning process than is our skill.

If every time we fail we took it personally, we would avoid failing. We would tend to play it "safe." We would not put ourselves in situations in which we may be terrible. If we couldn't make mistakes how could we learn? Are we somehow suppose to know how to be perfect, accomplished, masterful right from the start? The fact is you are the same person before you attempt to accomplish your goals, after the process is over whether you succeeded or failed, and during the process of learning.

When you can understand the profound implication of this principle, you can engage fully in your creative process and do the best you can. If you happen to fail while you are learning how to create the results you want, do it without a minor identity crisis.

In creating your life as art, it's important not to be seduced by success and fooled by failure. In my life, I have had both success and failure. I like the success much better than the failure. Often the success was a product of many failures while I learned what I needed to learn. Neither the success nor the failure defined who I am. I wasn't a better person when I succeeded. I wasn't a worse person when I failed. I was the same person, trying to create what was important to me.

We have to remember that in our lives many people and institutions have tried to manipulate us by linking our actions to our identity. Advertisers tell us we are better people if we use their brand of toothpaste. Schools tell students they are better people if they do all their homework and not as good people if they don't. Our families often try to shame us into better behavior by calling us names if we don't live up to their standards when we are kids.

It may take rethinking the relationship between what we think about ourselves and how well we are able to create the results we want for us to come to the understanding that there is no real connection other than the one we may manufacture. Another way of expressing this thought is this: we may create a fiction that we *are* what we do, but in reality, we are *not*.

Here's another thought experiment. Imagine yourself as a big success. Then imagine yourself as a big failure. And while you will enjoy the thought of success better than failure, realize that in both scenarios, *it is still you*…still the same values, same aspirations, same heart, same soul, same spirit, same loves, same hopes and dreams, same essence, same core of being.

From a practical point of view it is much easier for you to successfully accomplish your goals if you are not confusing yourself with what you do. You can be more objective, adjust your actions more easily, try out experiments, put yourself in a learning mode, and so on.

This principle is profound. If you can learn to adopt it, you will position yourself to be more effective and successful than you have ever been.

Principle 3:

Simplify when you can.

It could seem that I'm the worst person to give this advice. My life is not simple at all. I'm so interested in so many things that I get involved in all kinds of projects, organizations, causes, etc. So how can someone like me talk about simplicity without seeming a little hypocritical? Because, while I may be involved with many things, the complexity is only logistical, not spiritual.

Many busy people who have more complex lives than mine have a very simple and clear direction and solid foundation in their lives. If they didn't have such clarity, they would become overwhelmed. Some of us become overwhelmed without having that much complexity in our lives.

Perhaps you need to rework your logistics. Rethink your schedule, number of commitments, number of projects and activities you take on. Many of us think we can do more than we actually can. Sometimes things are more involved than we thought when we said yes to them. This area can be simplified rather easily.

But, more importantly, there may be an orientational dimension, mental, emotional, and spiritual dimension that needs clarity. We might say that life is not simple. Yet in some ways it is very simple. One very insightful view is that you are born, you have time on this planet, and then you leave. What is our life about while we are here? This is an age-old question, one that has been asked by every religion and school of philosophy. Can we really answer it to our satisfaction?

Deciding What's Really Important

There's the story of the man who couldn't find an answer to the question "what's it all about?" He had tried teacher after teacher, spiritual discipline after spiritual discipline, philosophy after philosophy. Nothing satisfied his question. He decided to commit suicide and end the question once and for all. But, just before he was about to do himself in, a friend came to tell him of a great sage he had heard about in the Himalayas. "This man is said to have all the answers to life's great mysteries. So, don't you think you should see him before you make this final fatal move?" Well, the man saw the logic of that argument, and off he went to seek out the sage. He got himself to the Himalayas by plane, train, bus, car, and then by foot. After days and days of climbing the most treacherous of paths, he came to a cave. He looked in the cave, and lo and behold, there was the famous sage he had sought. He slowly came before him, kneeled down, and respectfully asked his question. "People have said you have the answer to life," said the man. "That's right," the sage answered. "What is it?" asked the man. The sage smiled and then said, "Always agree with what anyone is saying." The man couldn't believe his ears. "No! No! It can't be that simple!" yelled the man. "Your right," said the sage. "It can't be that simple."

A life is made simple by adopting the principle of hierarchy. Life is very complex when we make everything equal. When things are of the same value, they naturally compete against each other for "air time" in our life. When we begin to sort out what's more important and what's less important, we begin to sort out the complexity.

Simplicity comes from clarity about what's important. For some people, their relationship with God defines their life. Everything else is a subset of that single experience. For others, relationship with loved ones is the most important aspect of their lives. For others, career, quality of life, helping others, or a sense of calling they have is the most important factor in their lives. Other things are subsets of their hierarchy.

Life is complex when we haven't defined what is important to us. Life is complex when we've made too many things important on an equal level. Life is complex when nothing in particular is important to us.

You can decide what is important to you. This is a major insight from Viktor Frankl's classic book *Man's Search for Meaning*. He came to understand that we decide or invent life's meaning. If we don't, we may be lost. For some of us, "inventing" is the right term to describe the meaning we give our lives. For others, a sense of "higher calling" is more the phrase that captures the essence of their lives. However, when we determine the highest position on the hierarchy, the theme in that position organizes our lives, although it is more accurate to say that we organize our life around it.

Frankl has said in his book *The Will To Meaning*:

> There is no place for value conflicts. However,
> the experience of the hierarchical order of

> values does not dispense man from decision-
> making. Man is pushed by drives. But he is
> pulled by values. He is always free to accept
> or to reject a value he is offered by a situa-
> tion.

What's your life about? This is not meant to be a deeply metaphysical or transcendental question. It is meant to be a clarifying
question. Perhaps a better way to phrase the question is what
have you decided to make your life about?

Make It Real

One caution: When you make your life about something you
think you need, but don't really care about, you become removed
from true meaning. You disconnect with your own deeper aspirations. Instead of simplifying your own life, life becomes more and
more complex.

If we choose to be a creator, then our mission is to give birth to
those things that we think matter. We make our lives about creating outcomes that we love, love enough to work on behalf of, sustain, and nurture.

People who spend their lives being against things can't think
in terms of their true aspirations. Perhaps they are against injustice. We applaud them for that. There is much real injustice in the
world. How can we best address it? From a problem solving point
of view, we attack it. From a creating point of view, we bring into
existence justice. To be against injustice is not enough if justice is
what we seek. We can build into our society a vision of justice, followed by the possibility of its manifestation. And then, as a secondary choice to that primary choice, fight against injustice
within the context of the real goal—justice.

No one understood this principle better that Martin Luther
King, Jr. He fought against injustice with great courage and
strength of character. Yet he understood that love is a more powerful force than hate. It was easier to mobilize people through
hate. Many tried and succeeded for a short time. But, learning his
lessons from Gandhi and Christ, he mobilized people through his
commitment to some of the highest principles there are—freedom, love, truth, fairness, righteousness, and justice. His love of

freedom and justice dominated the motivation of his movement. In some essential ways, his complex life was as clear and simple as it gets. Work toward the manifestation of love, truth, freedom, equality, and justice.

Simplicity Reveals Life's Poetry

Clarity about what you want to bring into being simplifies your life, while opening a source of strength to tackle all the secondary choices that may be needed to accomplish your goal. How do you reach such clarity? You decide for yourself what you will let your life be about. Your decision may be on the level of a great social cause, or it may be a very personal vision. Do not think that it must be momentous for it to be real. It only has to be what you want it to be. It is a gift to be simple. It is a burden to fill your life with meaningless complexity, which, in the end, will not seem important.

When someone dies, often what we remember are the small moments we had together. The time when she couldn't find her keys, the time when he found a book he was looking for at the library, the time she made coffee cake for a party and everyone raved, the time when he missed his plane but was able to get the later one, the time when she dialed your number by mistake but you ended up talking for an hour.

These are moments that we may not have noticed at the time they happened. Yet, they were recorded in our subconscious. We may have been unaware of how significant these precious moments were when they occurred, but we understand them in retrospect. Why did we not understand them at the time?

Often it is because we are filled with our grand concepts of what big things life is about. We can miss the poetry of the moment, the joy of the small, except when it's too late.

After my father suddenly died, my mother did something extraordinary. Just after the ambulance took him away, she went into the living room where they had several photo albums, collected through the years. She sat there for over an hour, looking at the pictures of their life together. She'd say, "And here's that time that we took that cruise to St. Vincent and he was so excited about the mangos we got on the beach…and look at this one, this was the time…" She was in shock, but she was also looking at their life from the lens of what was most real, important, and meaningful—those tens-of-thousands of little moments we often fail to notice while they are happening. We miss them because we are so distracted by the clutter of things that will turn out to be unimportant in the end.

We can train ourselves to see the great miracle that is before our eyes. We can tune our ear to the poetry of the ordinary moment in which nothing much seems to be happening. We can look at what's really there to see. And when we do, we can be thankful for every waking day. We can rethink our lives. We can experience the joy of living a life worth living on its own terms. We can come to a very simple truth: we have been given a gift, the gift of life. It is as simple as that.

Principle 4:

Don't look for the rules

Some people put their hopes in finding the right system, methodology, approach, rules, regulations, and regimen. They think that if they apply these rules, things will work out for them. They commit themselves to processes. To these people, how well they follow the rules becomes a test of their sincerity. They quote "higher authorities" such as authors, industry experts, specialists, and sages to establish the correctness of their approach. They become insecure when faced with people who can improvise, innovate, and break all the "rules" on their way to creating the results they want.

We are not talking about the wisdom of learning common practice and incorporating it into your own personal creative process. We are talking about what we could call the compliance equation: how well you comply with the rules is equal to how successful you should be. The degree to which you break the rules is the degree to which you will fail.

Once you establish structural tension, you may use conventional methods to accomplish your goal. But you may also use invention. Often you need to invent new processes, because your current reality lacks some of the things needed for conventional methods. In our corporate work, management teams often do not have enough time and money to use conventional methods to reach their goals. They have one of two choices: give up their goals, or invent new ways to achieve their goals.

My friend Terry Ortynsky owns several auto dealerships in Canada. He wanted to serve his customers better, more quickly, with higher quality service. His dealerships were set up like most in that there was a separate parts department and service department. When a mechanic needed parts, he had to place an order and then wait for the parts department to deliver it. This caused a delay for both the mechanic and customer.

Terry defined his goal as quick, convenient and high quality service for the customer, so he did something that was unheard of in his industry. He created a system in which the mechanics had their own inventory of parts and had easy access to them when needed. This was especially useful in the periodic service updates cars need. The time to service a car was cut in half, even as the quality rose dramatically.

Terry also measured how long it took a customer to complete all the paperwork when buying a car, paperwork such as registration, securing a loan, transferring ownership, etc. A customer was in an office an average of thirty-five minutes. But, after setting a new goal and looking at current reality, his management team cut the average time to less than seven minutes!

These are just two examples of a creator who invents in order to achieve his goals. These innovations were a product of structural tension, which included the realization that conventional methods couldn't get him where he wanted to go.

If you are a slave to convention, you are trapped within a rigid concept: There's a "right" way of doing something. There may be many right ways—i.e. ways that work. Also the so-called "right way" may not always work in your case. Do not become a slave to process. You may need to invent your own processes along the road to your goals, processes that no one else has ever imagined before. And the ones you invent may be better than ones you could have learned.

Creating the Long View in your Life

With these principles in mind, we can begin to think about the long-view.

Imagine your life twenty-five or thirty years from now. This can be a bit difficult for most of us at first. How can we do it?

It is helpful to leave out details. Our lives will take twists and turns we could never imagine. Sometimes we set out in one direction and years later end in a completely different direction. But there are a few things we may still count as important to us. We can divide the question of where we want to be long-term into two types of experiences. One is our internal life. The other is our external life.

The Inner Sketch

Our internal life is the far more important of the two. One can have wonderful surroundings, an affluent life style, good career opportunities, and other wonderful things in life, and still suffer insecurity, depression, lethargy, and hopelessness. On the other hand, one might not enjoy any of the benefits of a good material life, and still have peace of mind, involvement with life, and a sense of hope. External and internal conditions are independent from each other. And while we would want favorable conditions for both, let's understand that the internal counts more heavily than does the external in our overall experience of life.

How do you want your life to be far into the future from an internal perspective? What will be important to you? As you begin to form a picture of your future self, here are some things to consider: your state of being, your level of interest in what you may be doing, the love you have in your life, your involvement with others, the way you spend your time, your health, your sense of direction, your relationship with yourself, your relationship with your circle of friends and community. You might consider other factors of your internal life, such as your sense of spiritual fulfillment, your sense of commitment to your deepest values, your sense of direction, and your sense of place.

The ideas above are designed to set the stage for your sketch. Begin to image the inner life of your future self. How do you want to experience life at that stage? Probably you want it to be a good experience. Imagine that good experience now. Picture it; imagine how it will feel, imagine yourself there experiencing what you want in your future. (Thirty seconds to a few minutes of this is a good sketch.) This will be your first sketch. Do it now.

Two Roads

It seems that many people reach a point in life where the road has taken them to one of two different worlds. In one world, they have come to terms with their life. They feel they have come home to themselves. The other world is very different. In this world, people experience disappointment, resentment, anger, inertia, and hopelessness. They did the "right" things, but the promised rewards escaped them. They have lost out. They are stuck without any relief in sight.

The people in the darker world feel they have been dealt a raw deal. They may have thought that if they did the right things, accomplished the right goals, accumulated the right material goods, made enough money, etc., they would be happy. We must always understand that things do not make us happy.

The internal conditions you create drive everything else. If, in the long-term view of your life, you are free—free within your self, free within your life —you have reached a profound level of internal richness. There is an outer expression of freedom. Political freedom is a real factor in how we can organize our societies. There is a physical health dimension to freedom as well. As we get older, some of the physical freedom we once enjoyed may no longer be available to us. Yet, no matter what the outer circumstances, inner freedom can be available. It may include freedom to think what you will, freedom to love others, freedom to imagine, freedom to create. It may be an experience of freedom that is tangible but hard to put into words.

Another experience people have in the "lighter" world is a sense of peace of mind. Peace of mind is not the same as being in a constant state of tranquility and passive submission. Rather, it is a sense that, somehow, everything will be all right. Questions are either resolved or suspended. There is a rightness to things. The world, imperfect as it is, is worth being in. As Robert Frost said in his poem *Birches*, "Earth's the right place for love: I don't know where it's likely to go better."

Another dimension of peace of mind is a deeper connection with your own life, or higher consciousness, the Universe, or God, or nature. Peace of mind is a product not of suspension of conflict, but of involvement in those things that most deeply matter to you personally.

Regrets

Robert Frost, in one of his most startling insights, taught us much wisdom in his *West Running Brook*. This is a poem that describes the power of tension, of contrary motion, of things pushing against themselves. The poem is structured by a series of pairs. A man and a woman see a country brook, but rather than flowing east as most brooks do, this one runs west.

> "What does it think it's doing running west
> When all the other country brooks flow east
> To reach the ocean?…"

This question begins an exploration of the principle of contrasts and especially counterpoint. The couple notices a spray of water splashing against the current caused by a rock in the brook. That splash of water begins a dialogue in which the couple develops the idea that the nature of existence is not only the flow of the stream, but the instinct to go against the flow.

> "Speaking of contraries, see how the brook
> In that white wave runs counter to itself.
> It is from that in water we were from
> Long, long before we were from any creature."

The notion is that we have built into ourselves a dynamic of tension. Here's how Frost describes it:

> "It is this backward motion toward the source,
> Against the stream, the most we see ourselves in,
> The tribute of the current to the source.
> It is from this in nature we are from."

Earlier in the poem, Frost describes this movement of the stream this way:

> "Not just a swerving, but a throwing back,
> As if regret were in it and were sacred."

The notion that regret is sacred is a brilliant perception. The involvement we have with life must eventually lead to some regret. We usually think of regret as a bad experience. Yet, some forms of regret are inextricably tied to the exquisite nature of the best moments in your life. Our children grow up and move away. They are building their own lives, their own families, new friends, loves, interests. We want them to go. Yet, there is that tug at the heart when they move on. We remember them as young children their innocence, their trials, the sweetness of their nature. We wouldn't want them to stay ten years old forever. We want them to grow, mature, and learn to live their lives as best they can. But there is regret that a precious moment in our life is over now. This type of regret is sacred.

Not all regret is sacred. Some regret comes with bitterness, animosity, and exasperation. Life didn't turn out the way we wanted, and we somehow hold the universe responsible.

But sacred regret is sweet with a dash of pain built in. Sacred regret will be part of your long-view internal experience if your life has been filled with joy, love, and relationships. It will be there if you have had meaningful work and career. It will be there if you have had great adventures, made great products, served your community, and performed acts of kindness. It will be there because the precious moments of life flow down the stream of time, and yet our instinct is to move in counter motion against the stream toward the source.

Another Form of Regret

There is another form of regret. It is about those things we have done that we feel sorry about. For many years I had trouble understanding the Catholic Church's sacrament of confession. I puzzled over the idea that admitting you had done wrong would somehow change your opinion or relieve the burden you might be carrying. But, little by little, I began to get an inkling of the power of their approach. And you don't have to be a Catholic to understand the deeper principle that is embodied in the act of confession. We are imperfect. We make mistakes. Some of these failings are what we might call honest mistakes. We did our best, and we couldn't pull it off. These are the types of mistakes we learn from.

There is a different type of mistake. We failed, not because we tried and just didn't happen to succeed. Here, we failed to be true to ourselves, true to our values, true to what we thought was right. We may have thought we were right at the time, but in retrospect, we see we were terribly wrong.

Over the years, I notice myself thinking back to those types of moments in my life. Times when I said something that was hurtful. Times when I acted in ways that were unkind. Times that I could have been smarter, better, more understanding, more true to my values. Some of these regrets are from recent times, but some are very early transgressions.

There are thousands of such regrets we have. I think the Catholic Church has built into its system of spiritual development the need we have, as imperfect human beings, to forgive ourselves for our "sins," and renew our ability to turn over a new leaf. "Go and sin no more," is the phrase they use. As I've said, this principle is not just for Catholics. It is something we can learn from them. However we manage it, we need to put down the burdens we carry as we go forth in life. If we don't, the path gets heavier and harder to travel. Life becomes more of a burden than a blessing as we build up the load of unresolved regrets.

When you envision your future self, imagine yourself free of such burdens. Let them go. You do not need to develop amnesia. But you will no longer hold on to the memories as you once did. You will let them be what they were. You will get on with your life. You will be able to turn over a new leaf.

Structural Tension — Creating Your Internal Life

Let's experiment with structural tension using the type of internal goal we have been talking about. We continue to focus on the long-term internal state of being — twenty five to thirty year time frame, or whatever makes sense in your case. "Long-term" is the thought.

Think about the internal experience you want when you are at that stage of your life. Remember some of the principles we have explored. Do not problem solve, do not base your internal experience on a matter of identity, do not think in terms of rules about process, do not use perfection or suspension of human conflict as a standard of measurement.

Think about what you want to create independently from your sense of identity. Think about your sense of inner peace, sense of relationship with yourself and others, sense of involvement with your own life, sense of purpose, sense of meaning, and so on.

A Second Sketch

Use your first sketch as a starting point, but now refine it. In just a moment, picture your future self having created the inner state of being you want to create. Imagine how it feels, what quality it adds to your life, how simple and clear it is. Add anything else that you think is important. This will be your second sketch in creating your future self.

Close your eyes and picture this now (30 seconds to a few minutes.)

Now that you've imaged that state of being, let's think about current reality. What is your current inner state as compared to your desired inner state? Notice the ways you have achieved what you want and the ways that there is still a difference between what you have and what you want.

Close your eyes and focus on your internal state of being (30 seconds to a few minutes.)

You now have an idea about the outcome you want to create and your starting point.

The next step is to put them *together* in the same structure. In a moment, begin to imagine the desired future state, and, after thirty seconds or so, begin to add a picture of the current state. The best way to do this is a split screen image. At the top of the screen, picture your desired state. At the bottom of the screen, notice the current internal experience, and picture it there.

Hold these two images for a few minutes. As you do, notice the tension that is established by the difference between the current state and the desired state.

Remember to let your mind do the work. Do not attempt to resolve the tension, let your mind work this one out. You are simply stretching your bow and aiming your arrow. You are setting up your shot. You are positioning yourself well so you can reach your target.

Now that you know how to do the technique, give it a try.

The Long-Term External

While we can't predict what our life may be like in the long view, we can have some goals in mind. It's best to generalize about our future circumstances rather than attempt to put in many details.

You may have an idea about where you want to live or at least what type of place. Is it a tropical climate? Is it rural, urbane? Certainly you will want enough money to live in comfort. You will want to be healthy, interested in the activities with which you are involved. What do you want your life to look like, be like, and feel like? How are you spending your time? What are your interests? You will want people around you who you like or love. What else might be important to you?

The external conditions are only the logistics of your life. The external conditions are a container for the internal conditions. But, it's nice to have a container that is well suited to your life.

A general overview is all you need for this exercise. Don't try to add a great amount of details. You are answering the question, "What do I want in a longer time frame?"

Think about your current state as compared to your desired state. What about your living conditions? The people in your life? Your financial conditions? Your health? Your interests?

You can now establish structural tension. Focus on your vision of your life in the future. Then add to it your current reality as it relates to your long-term goals. Hold both images for a few minutes in a split screen mental picture—vision on top of the screen, current reality on the bottom.

Try this out now.

Creating Your Future

The ideas we have been exploring in this chapter are similar to a series of stretching exercises we might do before we do a workout or a jog. They warm us up, they put us in position to think about our life long-term, they give us a clear understanding of the difference between internal and external goals, and they enable us to think more clearly about what we might want the direction of our life to be.

There are many useful principles in this section that you can revisit throughout your life. A good rule-of-thumb is to rethink everything. And then soul search, be in touch with those things that matter most to you, and work toward creating your life around those very aspects you hold to be precious.

As we move to creating in a one-to-five year time frame in the next chapter, we can keep in mind our insights about our long-term aims. We can use many of the same principles in structuring our goals. We can better understand how our more immediate creative process connects with our long-term life direction.

The One and Five Year Plan

We have experimented with structural tension charting for short-term goals. We have considered the long-term direction of your life. And now we can begin to target your life for the next few years. For most people, a one-year time frame helps to define the major outcomes they want, the actions they need to take, and the overall strategy that might be helpful. A five-year interval is also useful.

A one and five year outlook, together, are both helpful and related to each other. As we work out the details for the one-year period, we know the major direction and benchmarks for the five-year period.

This thought process is not unlike how good pool players play. Not only do they sink the ball in the pocket, but they position the cue ball so that it is well placed to knock in many other balls. They are thinking about the relationship between the short term and the long term. And so should we.

From the Inner to the Outer

While most of the material in this chapter focuses on the mechanics of the creative process, we also need the right orientation and spirit. As we said in the last chapter, the inner life experience is more important than our external circumstances. Even though we want to create favorable outer conditions. And it is always good to remember that external things in our lives cannot make us happy for long.

Our initial work, then, is inner. But our creative process is not a form of problem solving in which we hope to solve the complexities of our lives by the success of our outer circumstances. Creating is not therapy. It is not a healing process. It is not a solution to your problems. Rather, it is a way to bring into being what you care about enough to dedicate your time, talents, and energy.

We certainly want a pleasing external life. Yet if we use the external to compensate for inner conflict, pain, confusion, and anxiety, we are hoping that our internal conditions will change *because* of our external situation. This is not a good platform for the creative process.

The internal life you create will more easily manifest itself outwardly than the other way around.

Quality of Life

Before you define the actual goals you want to create within the next year and five year periods, let's begin to think about the *quality* of your inner life during these periods. What do you want it to be? What is the feeling tone, the spirit, the involvement, the interests. You will want a sense of hope, a sense that it's good to be alive, a sense of love, and a sense of direction. These aspects of your inner life are qualities. They are not destinations one reaches but rather states of being one achieves.

As a creator, you can focus your generative direction on states of being as well as material goals, and if you do that before you consider major goals, you have a better foundation from which to create.

Take a moment, and imagine how you want to experience your life during this coming year.

And then the next 5 years.

Don't be surprised if the experience you want happens to be exactly the same for both periods. Often the inner states we desire do not change much.

Here's an exercise you can try: Close your eyes. Begin to imagine the internal state you want to create. Notice your current internal state. Focus on both states simultaneously from thirty seconds to a few minutes. Relax your focus. Open your eyes.

Giving your Mind Structural Tension

Remember: If you give your mind structural tension, it will begin to work out a strategy to accomplish this creation. Of course, you may need to take various actions. Structural tension will generate both inner change and outer actions that, together, enable you to achieve this internal state. As you repeat this exercise and take the needed actions, you will find that your internal experience quickly begins to be consistent with the state of being you want. Even if the external conditions haven't changed significantly at first, your inner state will. You will begin to experience a profound distinction between the outward circumstances, and the inner richness of your life. When this begins to happen, you begin to experience that the circumstances you happen to be in are not the driving force in your life — you are. And, this reorientation, from circumstantial to generative, puts you in a better position to create the outer circumstances you want.

Before you begin to think about the actual goals you may want to create this next year, think about the *context* in which these goals may be created. The context is the overall and general quality of your life. There is both an internal and external dimension to this. How are you spending your time? What kind of people do you have around you? What is your health situation? Your financial, professional, career situation? Remember, the way to answer these questions is by *quality* of life answers rather than actual goals at this point in the process.

Quality of life is *not* the same thing as life-style. You may be very focused on career, and because of this, you may need to travel as a secondary choice to support your primary choice. You may not like traveling. In this example, you may like the quality of life you have, but not like the life-style. You are organizing life-style to support the higher order goal of career. Even though you find that you need to travel, the quality of your life experience may be very consistent with what you want, both on the road and at home.

Your Goals

After you have thought about the overall quality of your life, begin to think about the major goals you would like to accomplish. For me, there are some very major things I want to accomplish every year. Perhaps it is a book I want to write, a film I want to shoot, an opera I want to compose, a new workshop or product I want to create. Sometimes it may be a new discovery that interests me, or something I want to learn. Years ago, one of my major goals was to teach myself to type properly. I am grateful to this day (even as I type these words) that I set out to achieve that goal.

All of the goals I have just talked about are goals around accomplishment. But there are other goals that are just as important and yet not in the realm of a major project or career achievement. Some goals concern my family: a visit by my son Ivan and his lady Jen, or sitting in the audience of my daughter Eve's school play. Thanksgiving, Christmas, and other holidays are precious moments that are important. These types of goals are just as meaningful to me as accomplishing an important professional milestone.

Setting Up Your Next Life-Phase

Think about this coming year. What changes do you want to create? What aspects of your life do you want to maintain or develop further? What outcomes do you want to achieve?

Think about this next five year period. What changes do you want to create? What aspects of your life do you want to maintain or develop further? What outcomes do you want to achieve?

Notice the relationship between the two. Is the one year period consistent with the five year period? What is the relationship? We want them to be consistent and compatible rather than in conflict. Make any adjustments you may need to so that these two time frames are aligned. In a moment, you will have a chance to define some of your goals. Before we do that, it is good to explore your general thinking about the relationship between our one year and five year creations.

Thinking About Goals

Remember to think in terms of the results you desire, and not in terms of problems you want to eliminate, nor the process steps that you might take. We are focusing our thinking, and the first focal point is the final outcomes we want to create

Take out a piece of paper, and list at least 10 "little" goals you want to create. This exercise has two functions: to identify some of the actual results you want to create, and to warm you up for the next list that will contain more involved goals. Okay, do this now. Now, make a new list. This time list 10 major goals that would be meaningful to you. The time frame for these goals is also one year. Some of your bigger goals may take longer than that, so you may want to think about the status of this longer-term goal one year from now. What needs to be in place by that time?

As you make your list, think about how it fits into your quality of life. It needs to be consistent with it. It can't be a contradiction to it, unless your goal is a secondary choice to a higher order primary choice that does support the quality of life you want to create.

List 5 to 10 goals for this next year.

List 5 to 10 goals for this next five year period.

Look at the relationship between both lists, and adjust as needed to make sure there are no conflicts of interests. Make sure that the shorter-term goals are consistent with your longer-term goals.

Refining Goals

Now that you have written a first draft of your two lists, here's a way to refine them. Check each item on your list against the suggestions below.

1. Form a mental picture of the results you described. Ask yourself: *Is this the result I want to create?*

If the answer is *yes*, you have described what you want. By going through the rest of this checklist, you will be able to refine your goals, and this will make it easier to organize your actions around them.

If the answer is *no*, then there is more work to do. Continue to describe the result you truly want to create. But don't get fooled into thinking that more and more details give you more and more information. Your goal should be broad rather than overly detailed, clear rather than vague, the overview rather than the minutia.

2. *Did you quantify the goal wherever you could?*

Whenever you can, assign actual numbers to your goals. It is easier to organize your actions when you know that the result is "5 new business clients" rather than "increased business." Aim your sights clearly and directly. To do this, you will need to make real decisions about what you want to create. Each time you put a number on an element that can be quantified, you define that element more clearly. It also gives you more clarity when later you define current reality. So get into the habit of assigning the actual numbers, and you will develop more precision and power in your ability to produce results.

3. Did you avoid comparative terms? If not, rewrite them.

Comparative terms such as "more," "better," "less," or "increased." These only have meaning when compared to something else. "Better health," for example, is a future desired state as compared to the present state. This description doesn't quite tell us what we want. For example, if your health is very bad, better health may still be inadequate. Inadequate health is not what you want to create! Rather than use comparative terms, describe the result you actually want, in this case: *Very good health.*

4. Are you creating results or solving problems?

Problem solving is taking action to have something go away, the problem. Creating results is taking action to have something come into being, the full achievement of your goals. If you write your goal from a problem solving point of view, you limit yourself to eliminating and avoiding, rather than creating and building. So, here is a major secret in creating the results you wants: Describe what you want to create rather than what you want to eliminate.

Here are some examples of this principle:

Rather than:

Overcome my weight problem

Write this:

I weigh 150 pounds

Rather than:

Fix the roof so it doesn't leak

Write this:

The roof is in perfect shape

Rather than:

Get rid of excessive work schedule

Write this:

Well-planed and executed work schedule with time to balance family and career

5. Are you describing a process or an actual result?

Process tells us the HOW, how do we accomplish our goals. End results tell us the WHAT, what do we want to accomplish. Process always serves an end result, that is its purpose. In the Master Chart, the end result should describe outcomes rather than processes — the WHAT rather than the HOW.

Here are some examples of these principles:

Rather than:

Run 4 miles every day

Write this:

A well-toned and healthy body

Rather than:

Get my significant other to agree to vacation

Write this:

A family vacation that everyone loves

Rather than:

Learn PhotoShop (a computer program)

Write this:

Mastery of PhotoShop

6. Are your goals specific or vague?

Make your end result specific rather than vague, and this will make it easier to organize around. As we said in the beginning of this checklist, a good rule of thumb is if an item on your list can be quantified, do so. When items are not so easily quantified, you can still apply this principle to be specific.

Look at both your one year and five year list of goals, and choose *one*. Make it one of the most important to you. This goal will be the subject of a "master" structural tension chart. The chart is a blueprint for action as well as a feedback system to track your progress. As you develop your structural tension chart, you will find yourself becoming clearer about what it will take to accomplish this goal. You will be better at assessing current reality as it changes, and you will be able to adjust your actions along the way as you learn from your involvement.

Building a Structural Tension Chart

The next step in our process is to build a structural tension chart around the goal you have chosen. We can work with this chart throughout our creative process. We can track our progress, update current reality, manage our due dates, and focus our mind's attention on the current state of structural tension. All of these actions are part of an entire dynamic in which the creative process generates momentum that propels us toward our goals. Some of our actions are very logical, and some of them are what we might call an "inner creation." We envision our end result, current reality, progress, learning, etc., and we become part of that dynamic process. As we maintain focus on our goals and current reality, we begin to assimilate the state of structural tension. Our minds begin to help us move to the resolution of the tension in favor of our desired outcomes. We find we have the energy we need to take all the needed action steps. We find that we suddenly have new ideas that enable us to work with greater efficiency and effectiveness. Coincidences begin to occur that greatly move us forward. We begin to sense a growing propulsion. We know we are on the move and on target.

To build a structural tension chart, choose one of your goals.

Think about your end result, and begin to describe its current reality. What do you have in place now in relationship to this result? Take a moment, and write a brief description of your current reality.

Do this now.

Checklist for Current Reality:

Now that you've defined your goal and defined its current reality, check your description against this helpful checklist. Refine your description as needed.

1. Did you use your goals as a reference point in describing current reality?

For example, if your goal is to build a vacation house, did you list the current situation such as financing, building skills, current property market, contractors in the area, etc.?

2. Have you described the relevant picture? and,

3. Have you included the whole picture?

For example, do we have a whole picture of the current state in relationship to our future state? It is always best when forming structural tension to think in pictures.

4. Translate assumptions and editorials into objective news reports.

Look out for assumptions that you may have built into current reality. Instead of assumptions, describe reality as objectively as you can.

5. Have you told the story without exaggeration?

Avoid exaggerations that describe reality either better than it really is, or worse than it is.

6. Did you state what reality is, or just how it got to be that way?

How reality got to be the way it is doesn't do the job. We need to know where we are right now. We may be able to learn from how we got to the current state, and that is good. But, in creating a structural tension chart, leave out the journey to current reality, and simply describe the place we have landed in this moment.

7. Have you included all of the facts you need?

There may be aspects of your goal that lead us to think about certain facts. If we have a weight goal, current reality will include our current weight. If we have a time goal, current reality may include how much time we have between now and our due date. Are there other facts that we need to give us an adequate picture of current reality as it actually is? If so, include them.

The Action Steps

Now that we have defined our goal and described our current reality, we are ready to map out our action plan. The best way to do this is to use the form we did for our short-term goals. The goal in a box on the top of the page, the current reality in a box on the bottom of the page, and between these two points, our action steps.

Once we have established structural tension, the natural question is, "How are we going to move from here to there?" As we think about the contrast, ideas begin to bubble. Some of these ideas are very obvious, and that is good. Often, many of our actions are the usual things we would have done anyway. Yet, in the context of structural tension, they take on greater focus and direction.

We also get many new ideas. Remember, once we establish structural tension, our minds are busily working to resolve the tension, and our spirit of innovation and creativity is contributing.

Ordinary and extraordinary ideas combine to answer the question, "How do I reach my goal?"

For this structural tension chart, do not list too much detail. Get the overview. After we construct this chart, we will see a way to develop detail for each of the steps, but in a way that doesn't overwhelm us. Right now, our action plan should be a blueprint of the overall shape of our actions, and not filled with too much detail.

At this point, make a structural tension form (goal on top, current reality on the bottom of the page), and then write in the action steps you will take to achieve your goal.

Okay, do that now.

Now that you have written your action steps, put a due date on each one. That will tell you *by when each step needs to have been accomplished* for you to create your goal in the time frame you want.

Date your action steps now.

Use the following checklist to refine your action steps.

Checklist for Action Steps:

1. *Ask yourself this test question:* **If we took these steps, would we achieve these results?**

The answer to this question is either YES or NO. If NO, then continue to fill in more action steps until the answer is YES. If the answer is YES, you have completed writing your action steps.

2. *Are your action steps accurate, brief, and concise?*

Sometimes people tend to write too much detail in their descriptions of actions. One or two short sentences usually are better than many long sentences. Be brief. Picture the action step. This will help you target it.

4. *Does every action step have a due date?*

Due dates add reality to your description of current reality. Due dates place each action into a time frame. If the action is accomplished by its due date, that action fits into the various actions that will create the goal.

Telescoping: the way to develop details

As we think about the structural tension chart we have just created, each action step describes a major action. But to accomplish each major action step, many other steps need to be taken.

How do we describe and organize these various activities? We could go crazy listing all the things we need to do because it can be quite overwhelming. So instead of driving ourselves to distraction, we will divide and think. We will separate our focus, first on our overview, and then on the necessary details. We will use a technique called telescoping.

What Is Telescoping?

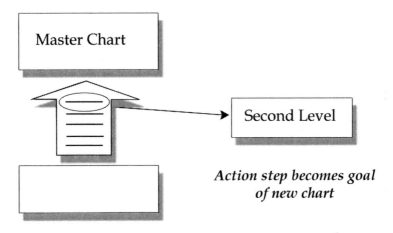

Action step becomes goal of new chart

Telescoping is just like it sounds, something smaller is contained within something larger. Each action step on the master chart becomes the *object of a new structural tension chart*:

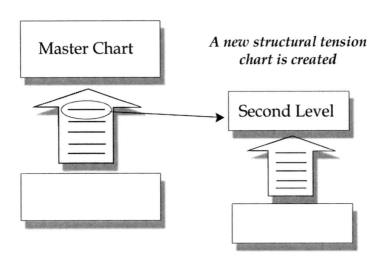

A new structural tension chart is created

When the action step becomes the goal of the new telescoped chart, we next describe its current reality, action steps, due dates and accountabilities:

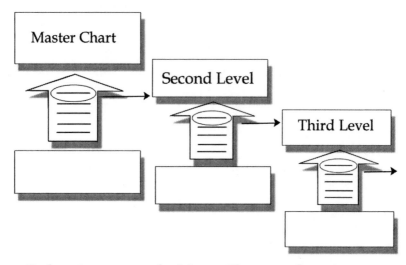

Each action step on the Master Chart may have its own structural tension chart. Each of the new second level charts may be further telescoped to third or fourth level charts, and so on. This is where the more exacting details are developed.

What Telescoping Produces

Telescoping is a fantastic way to keep track of the overview while managing the details. It gives us a feedback system, a tracking system, and a personal management tool that guides us through a comprehensive process toward our goals. Most projects have a master chart and one or two levels of action steps developed into other structural tension charts. Usually, we do not need a lot of charts for each project. But, with many projects or with especially complicated projects, we may find ourselves managing a lot of charts. When this becomes the case, you may want to use computer software to manage the charts.

Doing It On A Computer

One of the most convenient ways to construct structural tension charts is by using a computer. There is a particularly good software program that is designed to manage structural tension charts called *Alisar Charting*. It is a program that was created especially for the management and organizational world, and it was based on my book *The Path of Least Resistance for Managers*. The program can manage the structural tension charts for an entire organization, automate the tracking systems, tying lower level charts to their "parent" charts so that everyone can see the logic of the actions they are taking. It is a system that enables managers to have high levels of control of their management systems without having to micromanage the process.

Here is an example of a master structural tension chart that was constructed on *Alisar Charting*, and a second level chart.

MASTER CHART

End Result

Gift Basket Business: We create unique gift baskets that reflect the personality of the customer. The business is profitable and sustainable with sales of $500,000/year. Built from an in-home business to a small retail store. Our customers refer us to their contacts.

Action Steps

☐ My vendors work with me to locate unique gifts at a reasonable price	On Going	JS
☐ Introduce small store in trendy location	Year 4	JS
☐ Sales of $200,000/yr with corporate clients accounting for 60% of the sales	Year 3	JS
☐ Research potential locations for store	Year 2	JS
☐ Initial corporate sales of $20,000 with referrals to other corporate prospects	Year 2	JS
☐ Investigate local networking groups	Year 1	JS
☐ Initial offering Introduced for holiday business and teacher gifts	Year 1	JS
▣ Business start up	Two months	JS

Current Reality

I just moved to the city. I was a manager for a similar business in another city. Gifts and perks ranging from $20 - $100, that are in good taste, and taste good, are desirable for corporations, teachers and vendors. I want to work from home while my kids are small. My husband has a good job, so the risk is manageable.

SUBORDINATE CHART ⟵

End Result

Business Start Up (2 months) I can efficiently create and ship my initial offering. Functional assembly and storage area in our basement. Computer, bookkeeping program, phone and fax are at my finger tips.

Action Steps

☐ Set up the basement for assembly and storage	9/25	JS
☐ Set up books in small biz accounting	9/23	LJ
☐ Set up new e-mail account	9/23	LJ
☐ Order form created	9/17	JS
☐ Initial offering created	9/15	JS
☐ Locate vendors for cookies, wine, fruit, teacher gifts...	9/5	JS
☐ Name registered with state	9/1	JS
☐ Business strategy/plan complete	8/1	JS

Current Reality

I have a 2 month window of time to get the logistics of the business together. Our basement has room, but is not configured for the business. The phone and fax are in place. I have a computer. I have used a small business accounting program, but it is not on the computer. The order form has not been created. I have a basket vendor, but need to find fill products.

The first year it was released, the program was the gold winner in the 2002's *Lotusphere's* annual convention. *Lotus Advisor Magazine* said, "Looking for a new twist on planning and managing the goals of your organization? Look no further than *Alisar Charting*. This year's gold winner is a powerful idea put to good use...The tool captures strategic plans, project tasks, corporate vision, and even individual goals...If you've had trouble motivating your project team and making it clear how their efforts support the overall goals of the project, check out *Alisar Charting*." You can find out more about *Alisar Charting* on the web: http://www.alisarcharting.com

A Personal System

This system also can be used for personal structural tension charting. I find it useful when I am producing or directing a film project. There are many details that could be overlooked. That would be disastrous to the final outcome. So, tracking the master chart with due dates, and telescoping the various details that need attention from the master chart make the process more manageable than it would otherwise be.

Managing Structural Tension

Whether you use software or do it on paper, using structural tension charts can greatly increase your effectiveness. You can begin to manage your time, focus, energy, direction, and actions. Especially if the project you are creating is complex, the charts will track all of the relationships among the actions, track changes in current reality, show you your progress, and reinforce the inner state of structural tension by focusing your mind's attention. Using structural tension charts is more than creating a simple "to do" list. "To do" lists tend to drive our focus on single events. Structural tension charting enables us to see the relationship between the events we are taking and the overall context of the creative process.

"To do" lists focus our sense of time in the local and short-term time frame. Structural tension charting enables us to sense time dimensionally, so we experience the immediate moment and the longer term time frame we are in. This enables us to be innovative and creative within our own process. As we progress through a structural tension chart, we begin to see other ways we may accomplish our goal. We may be able to adjust our process, make it more efficient, and create an economy of means, so we are able to achieve our goals with an elegance that helps us do more with less.

Structural tension charting does one more very important thing. It generates a structure that has the most possibility to succeed, both short term and long term. But creating goals is more than a matter of mechanics. It is also a matter of orientation. In the next section of the book, we explore some of the most important insights there are for understanding why sometimes we accomplish our goals, only to have the success reversed over time. Good mechanics are essential. But so is creating the right underlying structures in our lives so that success becomes the platform for our life-building process.

Structural Imprinting

A Change of Structure—A Change of Life

In this next section of this book, we will explore the structural principles that can have some of the most important impact there is on your life. You will have a chance to probe your own structures and see how they influence you.

The defining question whenever we think about the structures in our lives is this: are your structures set up for success and advancement, or are they structured to produce a reversal to the success you have accomplished?

We have found the insights in this section to be some of the most original and important life-changing knowledge we have ever encountered. We have personally witnessed many thousands of people become able to rewrite their destinies, restructure their faulty reoccurring patterns, and reach a level of involvement and mastery in their own lives—changes that were simply impossible before they worked with this material.

This is not a section to be skimmed. These ideas, while easily understandable and completely logical, need to be digested. They need to be carefully thought through, pondered, analyzed, and contemplated. If you're a fast reader, it's a good idea to slow down a bit through this section. Make sure you let the ideas and their deeper implications sink in. This type of serious exploration will pay off exceedingly well. So fasten your seatbelt.

The Structural Patterns in Our Lives

In the 1938 movie *The Dawn Patrol*, Errol Flynn plays an easy-going World War I pilot who, with David Niven, his fun-loving buddy, flies dangerous missions during the day and carouses in town at night. He has another sport too: driving his overly serious squadron leader, Basil Rathbone, crazy. Ultimately, Rathbone takes revenge, for he so hates the Errol Flynn character that he names him the new squadron leader when Rathbone is transferred. Soon, Flynn begins to act as seriously as did the Rathbone character. His friend David Niven can't understand what's come over the Flynn character.

Now here's a movie that understands a common experience — *a position sometimes seems to dictate the behavior of the people who fill it more than the people themselves.*

Here is a pattern we see in many organizations, large and small: A person is not working well; management does everything to help improve performance, but to no avail. Finally, the person is replaced. Six months later, the replacement is performing exactly like his or her predecessor.

The Power of Structure

The pattern described above contradicts our most cherished ideas about human motivations.

How do we explain why people act the ways they do? It's their psychology, their DNA, their cultural background, their education, their life experiences, their values, aspirations, talents and abilities; their astrology, numerology, bio-rhythms; their age, gender, and generation. We test the potential and predisposition of employees before we hire them and track performance; yet, when it comes to replacements, though they are different in generation, gender, genetic code, temperament, experience, maturity, life situation, or work history, the pattern prevails.

The implication is that *no matter a person's individual traits, the structure of the position has a greater impact than any of those traits.* This is because structural dynamics is a more dominant force than any other factor in our make-up. The same principle is true for our personal lives. The underlying structures we are in are more influential in our lives than are our hopes, talents, experiences, knowledge, aspirations, values, and good intentions.

We are structure-seeking beings. We consist of structure, we gravitate to structure, we are motivated by structure, we respond to structure, we react to structure, and we resonate to structure.

That is not to say that we usually recognize the structures in our lives. Most structures are invisible to us on a conscious level. But, on a subconscious level structure is perceived and comprehended in some very essential ways.

Even though normally the structural dynamics in our lives are invisible, structure is a primal instinct. The audience rejects a film that is not well structured, the reader finds it hard to follow a book that is not well structured, the potential customer's attention is difficult to grab if an ad is not well structured. That is why filmmakers, writers, and ad designers are structuralists—people who use structural dynamics in their work.

What they understand is that the human psyche is attuned to structure. Without proper structure, communication, expression, and logic would be very difficult to master. Language itself is primarily an invention of structure. Sentences have structural relationships of nouns and verbs, and modifiers that orchestrate these relationships. We think in structures, dream in structures, see, hear, taste, smell, and touch in structures.

Since the basic unit of structure is the tension-resolution system, we can see how various forms of tension dominate the human experience. Sexual experience is a structural rendezvous of tension-resolution, as is eating and drinking. All sports are tension-resolution systems. One of the most basic sports is prize-fighting. The tension consists of two hopefully equally matched boxers who try to defeat each other. From the spectator's point of view, who will win and who will lose is the basic tension, which is resolved by the outcome of the fight. From the boxers point of view, how much to attack and how much to defend against the opponent's attacks are strategy questions which are tension-resolution systems. Football, baseball, basketball and all such team-against-team sports have the same basic structure, the same basic tension-resolution system for the spectators. The set of rules of each sport is a unique form in which the universal structure can play itself out. Would the spectators be as interested in a less structured free-for-all, or in an activity in which there was nothing to overcome, no contest, no tension? Not at all. Even individual sports in which there may be no contest have the form of the person against the elements, his or her personal best, or even the challenge to one's inner strength and character.

A stronger way of expressing this idea about structure is this: *We are imprinted with structural dynamics.*

The birth cycle is a tension-resolution system. But even before that, unborn babies respond to such structural input as music, poetry, the mother's speech patterns, and other such stimulus. Infants respond to the most basic rhythms, and this is partly due to the first stimulation of the mother's heartbeat. The heartbeat is both a physical tension-resolution system, and a musical tension-resolution system, consisting of the complex rhythm of an iambic phrase: short-long, short-long, short-long.

Robert Frost thought language was not only a product of the structure of nouns and verbs, but of sound itself. He talked about "sound sense," which was the ability of voice inflection alone to carry meaning. To prove his point to a friend he was with, he shouted to a farmer they saw in a far off field. Frost made the inflection of "Hi! How are you today?" but using gibberish rather than words. The farmer shouted back, "Fine, and how are you?"

Not only do language and sound have structures, but so do our lives. Our life structures have a profound impact on us.

Without exploring your own life-structures, the aim of creating the life you want may be improbable, for the wrong structures lead us to oscillating patterns in which success is eventually neutralized. Yet, the right structures enable us to build our lives on a solid foundation.

The Design a Life Makes

Poor Orson Welles. If you read any of the many biographies of his life, (one of my favorites is Barbara Leaming's *Orson Welles*) you see him cast as a character caught in the same film, over and over. He would wander into identical types of situations, having the same shape and form, the same beginning, middle, and ending, the same critical points in which, in the end, success was turned into failure. There is no doubt about his absolute genius, a word that is used so promiscuously these days that it almost loses its meaning. Welles was a genuine and unique genius. Except the same unfortunate pattern kept repeating itself in his life.

The pattern was rather like the plot of *Citizen Kane*, his first great cinematic masterpiece. It is the story of a boy who is snatched away from innocence and thrust into a position of great power and wealth, only systematically to fall from grace into a kind of wealthy poverty and powerlessness. Welles called *Citizen Kane* the great American failure story.

We all have a form of Orson Welles built into the circuitry. And we also have a success pattern built in as well. One thing that we can learn from biographies is that even the most accomplished among us has high points and low points in their lives. There are special rhythms and cycles. There are patterns unique to the individual that are like a dance that repeats itself in many guises. Each person's life has a remarkable and recurring design.

When we are very close to the events of our lives, we can't see the design. But when we back up, view these events from a greater perspective and distance, the design becomes clear. We begin to see predictable patterns in our lives. The details of the events we live through are unique and unlike any of the events that have ever happened to us. But the plot is often identical, repeating itself yet again.

Macrostructural Patterns

In fact, my first major discovery about structure and its impact on people was by observing how the events of our lives follow predictable patterns.

I was on the phone with a friend who I hadn't talked to for over six months. The last time I had talked to him, he had just begun a new relationship. At that time he was very excited about his "new woman." But now the relationship was over. "What happened?" I asked. He began to tell me.

Since I was at my desk, paper and pen close at hand, I began to jot down the major steps he was describing. They had been introduced by a friend. He asked her out on a date, but she was hesitant. After a few more calls and invitations, she finally said yes and agreed to have dinner with him. The evening was a big success for both of them. It turned out that they had a lot in common, interests, tastes, values, and life experiences. They both had just left a relationship. They both wanted involvement with another person. They both were interested in sports, running, sailing, exercise, biking. They both loved nature. They both loved camping in the woods. They loved the same kind of music and films. And they seemed to like each other.

When I had talked to my friend six months earlier, he was smitten. He was convinced he had found the soul mate he had been searching for his whole life. And that first period was like a dream come true for both of them. But as time passed there were some complications and reversals.

She began asking him to make himself available to her more than he was able. His work required him to travel quite a bit. Because of his schedule, he couldn't be with her for important social events. He complained that she wasn't supportive of his career. She complained that he wasn't emotionally available to her when he was there. They had a period of disillusionment, and they stopped seeing each other for a while. But they began to miss each other. She called and invited him over to her place for dinner. They got back together, and it was good again. But then came a new complication: He met another woman. He dated this new woman a few times, but this relationship wasn't very serious.

Of course, his lady became jealous and possessive. She asked him for a greater commitment in the relationship. He agreed and stopped seeing the other woman. Things went well for a few weeks, but he began to resent what he saw as her attempt to control him. They would argue. They would make up. They would fight again. They would make up again, each time thinking that this time would be different, and they would be able to build the relationship. Finally, she asked him to marry her. He said he had to think about it. He stopped calling her, and told her he was busy with work. Then she called him and they had an enormous fight. She called it quits. The relationship was over.

As he told me the story, I realized, while it wasn't very nice for either one of them, the story itself had a very solid structure. In fact, it had almost a musical structure.

Form and Analysis

In conservatories of music, student composers study "form and analysis." Students analyze various pieces of music so they can learn how to see the form and structure that composers used in writing pieces. Sometimes the students analyze a piece by Mozart or Beethoven, sometimes a piece by Corelli or Poulenc.

I had taken two years of form and analysis as an undergraduate at the Boston Conservatory, and two years of graduate level work in my post-graduate studies. Later, I had taught form and analysis at the college level. So it was quite natural for me to look at a story like my friend's and begin to analyze its form as if it were a piece of music.

Like all music, it had a beginning, a middle, and an end. But there were aspects of his story that were unique to him. In fact, as he was telling me the story of his relationship, the form seemed similar to other stories he had told me in the past about his life.

The blocks I had written down were these:

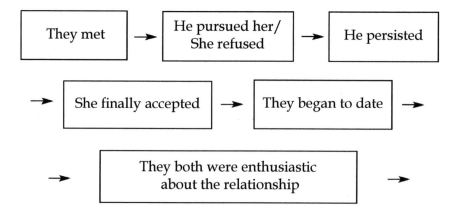

→ | He was busy with his career | → | She wanted more of his time | →

→ | He felt unsupported | → | She felt he was unavailable | →

→ | Both felt disillusioned | → | They stopped seeing each other | →

→ | They missed each other | → | They got back together | →

→ | Things were good | → | He began seeing another woman | →

→ | She became jealous and possessive | → | She asked him for a greater commitment | →

→ | He agreed/stopped seeing the other woman | → | Things went well for a few weeks | →

→ | He began to resent her | → | They would argue | →

→ | They would make up | → | They would fight | →

→ | They would make up again | → | She asked him to marry her | →

→ | He stopped calling her | →

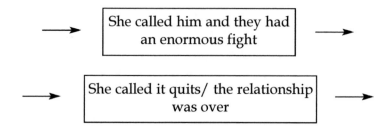

A translation from the unique to the general

I translated the story from the specific event that happened, to a general description of the type of event that it was. Here's how I described it:

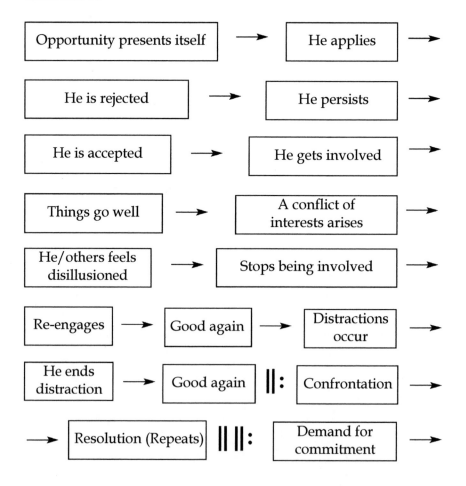

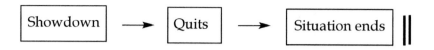

Having written this description, I asked my friend to think about another relationship he had had. I asked these questions:

Did an opportunity present itself?
Yes.
Did you apply?
Yes.
Were you rejected?
Yes.
Did you persist?
Yes.
Did she then say yes?
Yes.
Did you then get involved?
Yes.
Did things go well for a time?
Yes.
Was there then a conflict of interests?
Yes.
Did you or the other person feel disillusioned?
We both did.
Did you stop being involved?
Yes.
Did you then get back together?
Yes.
Was it good again.
Yes.
Did a distraction occur?
Yes.
Did you end the distraction?
Yes.
Was it good again?
Yes.
Was there then a series of arguments followed by making up?
Yes.

Was there then a demand for commitment?
Yes, but this time I asked her to marry me.
What happened then?
She said she didn't want to get married.
Did you then have a showdown?
Big time and she broke up with me.
So she quit?
Yes.
And the relationship was over?
Yes.

At this point I was getting pretty excited. Every step in the pattern had happened in the same sequence of steps. The only differences were who took some of the steps. For example, in the first story she asked him to marry her. In the second story he asked her to marry him. I asked my friend how long the first story took place. He told me five months. I asked him how long the second story took place, and he told me three years. So the same pattern played itself out, but in different blocks of time.

I then asked my friend to think of other times he had set out for a result, had it for a period of time, but didn't have it at the end of the story. I asked him to think about stories that didn't involve relationships because I wanted to see if this pattern existed in other areas of his life. We tracked several jobs and projects, building a house, going on vacation, and going on a diet. With each story I asked him if each step had happened. Did an opportunity arise? Did you apply? Was it first rejected?, etc. The answer was always yes. In every case he had lived through the identical pattern. In some cases he was the person to take a particular step. In other cases, someone else took the step. It didn't seem to matter to the design of the pattern who took the step, but that the step occurred in the same sequence. Somehow it was built into the pattern.

The time frame for each story ranged from only a few days, to some stories that took place over ten or more years. Later work on patterns demonstrated that the same pattern could happen in a matter of minutes, or over a period of twenty or more years such as in a marriage or job.

For the next few weeks I constructed the patterns of everyone I knew. I found that there were two distinct types of patterns, successful ones and unsuccessful ones.

The successful ones had their own style and rhythm. But in these patterns, unlike the unsuccessful ones, success was reinforced rather than reversed.

The successful patterns became building blocks for further success. They advanced.

The unsuccessful patterns oscillated. In them, success would always be neutralized and reversed.

For many years after that day on the phone with my friend the questions that I studied were *why do these patterns exist? How can we change the oscillating ones? How can we build on the successful advancing ones?*

Within the first six months of this discovery, I led the first workshop on *Macrostructural Patterns*, the name I had given them.

The word macrostructural comes from music. It describes the overriding structure of a piece of music. Macro, as contrasted with micro, describes the overall and larger view of something. In this case, the term Macrostructural Pattern is well suited to direct our attention to the larger shapes of our life.

The Difficulty in Changing Patterns

My first, but very naive idea, was that the best way to help people change their pattern was to tell them about the patterns — especially their unsuccessful ones. If they knew the larger shape, they would not be fooled by the events that they were experiencing. They could make better choices rather than simply react to the circumstances in which they found themselves. At least this was my hope. Since this should be an easy matter, I had scheduled the workshop for only one 9-5 day.

The room had about forty-five participants in it. I began to talk about the discovery, and then I led people through a process in which they constructed their oscillating Macrostructural Pattern. Everyone was able to do that. But as we progressed, the room seemed to shake. People got upset, depressed, angry, hopeless, irritable, downcast, and very, very heavy. What had happened was this. When they saw their oscillating pattern, most of the participants felt doomed and confronted.

They felt doomed because, having looked at the pattern, much of their lives seemed predestined to fail. Many of them were right in the middle of their patterns in their relationships or careers, and they saw that the next series of steps would be a repeat of the same failure they had seen in other parts of their lives.

Many of them felt confronted because the pattern contradicted the explanations they had about the stories of their lives.

The pattern seemed to rub their noses in the reality that more was going on than they had every imagined. That they weren't victims of circumstances or other people's transgressions after all. I remember one outraged woman complaining that the pattern contradicted her way of dramatizing her divorce, particularly the villainization of her former husband. She wasn't alone in what she was seeing.

The room got warmer and warmer, and I thought to myself, "What the hell is going on? Are these people all crazy?" I then presented the advancing structure, and soon people saw that they had a pattern that *did* enable them to create goals successfully. But most of these people still felt unresolved conflict about many of the events of their lives. I learned a lot that day.

I learned that seeing one's macrostructural pattern doesn't actually change the pattern. If anything, it can drive people a bit crazy. I also saw that people could be in love with their explanations of the events of their lives, so much so, that it's hard for them to consider other possibilities objectively.

Over years of having helped thousands of people construct their macrostructural patterns, I also learned the difference between young people and adults in their reaction to knowing about their oscillating patterns.

Adults often feel confronted by knowing there has been a predictable force in their lives that has been in play. Young people often feel the exact opposite. They are glad to know that there has been a real dynamic in operation, and the events of their lives are not arbitrary. They are glad to know the world makes more sense than it had seemed.

As adults, we create myths about ourselves and about our lives. We often use the myth to organize reality into a type of order. Anything that might contradict the myth seems to bring disorder that can feel disorienting. The myth forms a bias and matrix against which the person's life experiences are evaluated. The sense of myth is often in sharp contrast to the macrostructural patterns that dominate our lives. The myths are often about the details of the events that happened, including who did what to whom. The pattern shows that the details are not causal but only orchestrative. If we describe the details, we see the uniqueness of the events that have taken place, and the story can seem like a "one time deal." But if we describe the form and sequence of events, the critical moments, etc., we see how un-unique the story actually is. We can see that, yet again, the same damn thing has happened.

What Causes the Patterns

Why do these patterns exist and why do they repeat themselves? These questions led me to still deeper questions, deeper observations, and a deeper understanding. In the case of this exploration, *all roads led to structure*.

Structure has a goal. The goal is equilibrium. Structure wants all elements within it to be equal. When they are not equal, structure strives to change the situation and make them equal.

When I say "structure wants..." I don't mean to imply that structure has a mind or a wish or a desire. The force is impersonal. It is the same to say that gravity wants to attract the biggest masses to itself. We are describing a force of nature and not some psychological notion.

Nonetheless, structure wants non-equilibrium to end and equilibrium to be established. Any structure that contains non-equilibrium has a built-in dynamic for change, and this dynamic generates a tendency for behavior.

For us, equilibrium is not a better state than non-equilibrium. We don't mind when things are not equal. *But structure does*. This is why we can use this fact strategically when we deliberately set up structural tension. The difference between our goals and current reality creates a state of non-equilibrium. The structure moves toward restoring equilibrium, which happens when we accomplish our goal. At that point, the actual state is equal to the desired state. In reality, we have what we want, and structurally, equilibrium is established.

So How Come We Have Oscillating Patterns?

Structural tension is a "simple" structure. That is not to say that structural tension always is easy to form. The challenge is in the great discipline and skill it often takes, not in its complexity.

Some of the skills are those of knowing how to think about your goals. Some of the skills concern how to discern reality accurately. Some of the skills are how to take strategic actions, learn from the experiences, and make hard choices.

But as a *structure*, structural tension is simple in that it has a *single* dominant tension, which is fully resolvable. Once the tension is resolved, there isn't any other dynamic pulling you away from maintaining the success you have created.

Oscillation is produced by a more complex structure.

One way to think about it is this: imagine that you love pickles. But pickles make you sick. Every time you reach for a pickle you have a mix of desires and feelings. You want to eat this big delicious green thing that seems to be beckoning to you. But you can remember the last time you had that great half-sour dill, and the night of cramps that kept you awake until four-thirty in the morning. You may think, "a little bite won't hurt me. After all, last time I had three of them."

Two pickles later you are beginning to shift your thoughts from the great flavor experience you are enjoying, to images of another late night adventure in pain and suffering.

In this little example we can see the form of an oscillating pattern. There are *competing* forces in play. The love and desire for pickles is one force. An aversion to pain is another.

Competing Forces Leads to Oscillation

In oscillating patterns there are at least two major forces in play. One is a desire for something...usually a goal, a result, or an outcome. However, built into the system is another factor, which somehow says, "it's *not* okay to have what you want."

Why it's "not okay" is different for different people in different structures.

In some structures it's not okay to have what you want because you think you are unworthy of success. In some, it's because you fear that bad things will happen if you are successful. In some cases it's not okay to have what you want because there are other people in the world who are suffering, and why should you be better off than they are? In some cases it's not okay to have what you want because it doesn't serve to justify your existence, and somehow it seems important to justify one's life by doing altruistic deeds.

Many such factors are built into an individual's structure. We call these types of structural elements *conceptual complexes.*

Here are three different elements that combine within a more complex oscillating structure: *desire, goal, or vision; the current real - ity; and a concept that contains the notion that it's not okay to have what you want.*

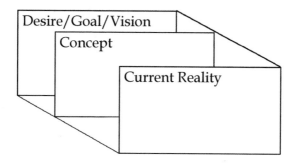

When these three factors are in the same structure a natural competition emerges. As you begin to move toward what you want to create, at first the two most pronounced factors are your goal and your current reality. Vision and Current Reality form one tension-resolution system within the structure.

As you begin to make progress toward your goal, however, the contrast between the desired state and the actual state diminishes. The tension between them is resolving. But as that happens, another tension-resolution system built into the structure begins to increase. That is the tension (or difference) between having the result you want (which is fast becoming Current Reality,) and the concept that it's not a good thing to have what you want. This is the pickle-pain principle.

In my *Path of Least Resistance* books, I have illustrated this principle by a diagram of a person between two walls. The person has two different rubber bands connected to him that represents two different tension-resolution systems within the same structure. One rubber band is tied to the wall in front of him; the other to the wall behind him. Each rubber band is a separate system, but systems that are connected to each other within the same unified structure.

In reality, sometimes you are closer to one wall, and sometimes you are closer to the other.

The wall in front of him has VISION written on it. The wall behind him is marked CONCEPT: you can't have what you want.

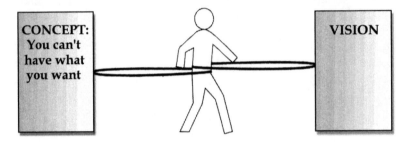

As the person begins to move toward his vision, the rubber band in front of him relaxes. But the rubber band behind him is stretching tighter and tighter.

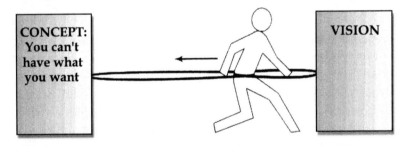

Within this structure, the dominant tension-resolution system is the contrast between having the result you want, and the concept that it's not okay to have it. The longer you live with the result, the more the tension builds. Your mind is trying to resolve the growing trepidation that the current situation produces. The structure strives to resolve the non-equilibrium.

The phrase *The Path of Least Resistance* refers to the principle in nature that energy moves where it is easiest for it to go. Looking at this diagram, we can see that the place where it's easiest to go within this structure is away from the situation of having the result. And that's what we find in the oscillating pattern. Having achieved a result, the person is unable to keep it. There will be a reversal.

The structure has been in a state of pronounced non-equilibrium. But now it is restoring equilibrium. And remember, that is *its* goal. We could say that in producing this reversal, the structure is just doing its job.

As the person moves away from the accomplishment of his vision, there is a new shift of dominance within the two competing tension-resolution systems. As reality moves away from the desired result, and the desire doesn't go away, the new dominant tension is once again the contrast between the desired state and the actual state.

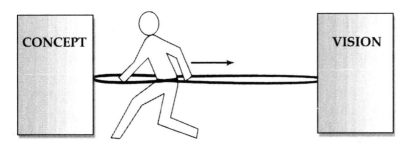

The actual goal may no longer be desired. But the type of goal may still be very much in play. The person may no longer want a relationship with the person they just divorced, but they may still want a loving relationship.

In fact, this type of pattern often is filled with irony. I have known people who, at the end of a cycle of oscillation with a relationship, swore off any new involvement. Usually a day after making this pronouncement, they met a new love interest that knocks them off their feet. The day after that, they are back in the pattern.

Structure's Goal of Equilibrium

The goal of the structure is to have equal tension between the rubber band in front and the rubber band in back, i.e. equilibrium.

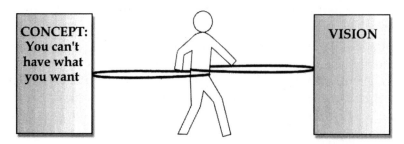

The structure's goal is not our goal. We want to have what we want. But having what we want is a condition that produces the state of most *non-equilibrium*.

Here is a technical way to show the power of this structural dynamic:

> The event:
> Having the result you want

- Within a success pattern that is the point of *perfect equilibri - um*. (Imagine all rubber bands relaxed.)

- Within an oscillating pattern that is the point of *most non- equilibrium*. (Imagine one rubber band is fully stretched and at its point of most tension.)

Experiments Addressing Oscillating Patterns

After I discovered the macrostructural patterns, I tried many approaches to overcome them. I first tried to "cut" the other rub- ber band. I tried to change the person's essential beliefs or con- cepts. What I found was revelatory for me and deeply troubling for people who do "belief work." *People most often do not change their most deeply ingrained beliefs and concepts.* If the belief doesn't change, then trying to "cut that rubber band" isn't possible.

Another approach I tried was *pattern interruption.* If you know the typical step in the pattern, do something vastly different from the type of action you would usually take at that step in the cycle. If on step six you always avoided a confrontation, instead, this time, have the confrontation. If in step four you always jumped into a project, mind, body, and soul, this time be more circumspect and hesitant.

What I learned from these experiments was that individual steps could be changed within the cycle—people could indeed change the nature of the step—but the overall pattern would still continue. The cycle of oscillation didn't change at all. Success was still neutralized and reversed. The outcome didn't change. Even though a step or two might have been different, the rest of the pattern stayed intact

The Wasted Attempts of Trying to Change Beliefs

Usually people attempt to change beliefs and concepts by affirmation or argument.

The affirmation approach attempts to "reprogram" the subconscious mind. This idea is similar to reprogramming a computer. It is hoped that a new belief can be rewritten over an old one, and the subconscious will be guided by the new belief. If you thought you were stupid, you would affirm that you are smart. If you believed you were undeserving of success, you would affirm that you deserve great and wonderful things to happen to you. If you believed you were "weak-willed", you would affirm that you have great determination and commitment.

There are many reasons why beliefs do not change by affirming the beliefs you like. One of the most compelling is that the attempt to reprogram the belief itself ironically *reinforces* the belief. We could call this the *boomerang effect*. Who, but a person who thought that he was stupid, would be affirming how smart he was? Who, but a person who believed she was undeserving, would be attempting to convince herself how deserving she was? Who, but a person who thought he was weak, would be trying to drum the idea of determination and commitment into his brain?

Another approach toward changing beliefs or concepts is by argument. A case would be made to refute the concept. If a person thought that he or she was a coward, the person would try to create a series of experience to demonstrate bravery, such as sky diving, competing in treacherous motorcycles races, practicing extreme skiing, and engaging in other daredevil feats. All the years of collecting such experiences would surely prove that the person was not a coward. After all, look at all the examples of bravery. But the irony is that all of the experiences point back and reinforce the original belief rather than contradict it. It's that old killer boomerang effect again.

The motivation of this approach tells the whole story. Why is the person collecting experiences of bravery to put into the catalogue? How are they trying to define the meaning of these experiences? Who, but a person who thought he or she is a coward, would need to prove that it wasn't true? All of the examples of bravery show that proof was needed, so, therefore, bravery must be in serious doubt.

You Create Your Life

You create your own life. That's not to say that you create all the various circumstances of your life, nor does it mean you have an understanding of just how you create your life. The statement simply means that when all is said and done, you are the central figure in the outcome.

Now, this notion, that one creates his or her life, has become a popular idea in the last number of decades. The only trouble is that many of the ideas about just how you do create your life are often reduced to very simple concepts about *belief*. The idea is that "belief creates reality." Because people believe something to be true, their experiences tend to move in that direction. The message is this: to change your life, change your beliefs. You need to think well of yourself, if you don't happen to, or you need to develop a positive predisposition about the future, or you need to work on beliefs that contradict the outcomes you want to produce. Your job, in this scenario, is to be the traffic cop for your various beliefs, letting the desirable ones move ahead, and stopping those beliefs that contradict your goals.

A lot of people have tried to take this approach over the years. They have tried to organize their belief system by holding beliefs that they thought would aim them toward their desired goals. They also have tried to manufacture beliefs that they thought necessary for success. For example, if they thought themselves unworthy of success, they would try to convince themselves they were worthy. If they thought they weren't smart enough, they would try to convince themselves that they were smart. Each "negative" would be addressed by a "positive." They tried to indoctrinate themselves by affirming the "positive" beliefs. They hoped they were "reprogramming" their subconscious minds, which would then manifest the outcomes they desired.

If you buy the hypothesis, you probably will buy the action plan. One begets the other, because people do really want to create the lives they want. But, trying to change one's beliefs doesn't lead to overall success. Instead, it leads to an oscillating pattern.

The pattern is usually this: work on your beliefs, have some positive changes, feel encouraged, generate some success…(so far, so good.) But then there comes a reversal. Something happens that moves you away from the result you want…a crisis, a problem, an unexpected event, a conflict of interests, becoming bored, unanticipated negative consequences, etc. Then you work some more on your beliefs since you think that your beliefs caused the reversal.

You become more internally referential. Rather than evaluate how things are going based on how close you are to creating the results you are after, you begin to look for how consistent is your belief system. Often you begin to obsess about your "hidden" beliefs (what you might believe but don't know you believe,) and then you put your random thoughts under the microscope. Eventually you seem to be losing the battle. The power to create what you want eludes you, and you can't do much about it, except try to manipulate your beliefs. After the episode is over, you still have other goals. To prepare, you look at your belief system again to make sure there is a better chance of success. Again, the same oscillating pattern happens, with success often achieved temporarily, but not able to be maintained.

To see if you have this type of pattern, track the successful events of your life and notice what follows them. Do they end well, or are there reversals after the successes, ones that make it hard or impossible to continue to maintain the successes you have achieved?

In our studies of structural dynamics, we have seen this type of oscillating pattern play itself out time and again. But the pattern can be confusing when you're in it. After all, some of the time you are moving in the direction you want to go. The pattern often includes successful accomplishment before the reversal comes.

The Curse of Sanity

You can't always just decide what you will or will not believe. The reason is that most of us suffer from the curse of sanity. We are sane in the sense that we can observe reality. If we see a bird, we can't force ourselves to think that it's a dog or a car or a CD player or a swimming pool.

As human beings, however, we have the bad habit of creating symbols out of things. If we see a bird, we can say it's a sign of good fortune, or a sign of death, or a sign of Spring. We often mix our observations together with our speculations, and we can get muddled. But something inside of us, if we are sane, will not let us get away with too much of that. There's a point where the mind rejects the hypothesis we are trying to impose on it and fires back with iconoclastic fury. "It's a bird. The Emperor has no clothes. A rose is a rose. Cut the shit."

If you tried to create your life by managing your beliefs, you would create a conflict between the beliefs, on the one hand, and the mind's unreasonable insistence on sanity, on the other. As you tell yourself that the bird is a swimming pool, your mind automatically rejects the idea. The inner thought process might be a little like this:

YOU
"That thing that looks like a bird is really a swimming pool."

YOUR MIND
"Bullshit."

YOU
"It really is."

YOUR MIND
"Bullshit."

YOU
"When I look at it I can picture it as a swimming pool, and therefore it must be a…"

YOUR MIND
"Bullshit."

The more we try to impose beliefs on ourselves that are contradicted by the reality we observe, the more the mind will fight against it. Pop-psychology and the positive thinking movement have long argued that the mind will move in the direction of those images you feed it. But they never took into consideration the mind's predisposition toward sanity nor the human value of truth as a living, vital factor in our make-up. Yes, people can be brain washed. But the brain needs intensive "washing" for the mind to adopt beliefs that are inconsistent with reality. In fact, one brain washing technique is to discredit reality as a frame of reference. This has to be done because the mind continually observes reality as it is, and the obvious contradictions create enormous discrepancies.

The conflict between what we might like to believe and what we see can be intensified when we try to force the mind to accept beliefs it doesn't perceive to be true. Then there is a breakdown of our relationship with ourselves. People begin to feel "inauthentic." They can't trust themselves. They become confused, unclear, trying to break away from the rut that they have backed into. Belief becomes superstition. To hold the right beliefs is to hold the right magical talisman. But, as time moves, it is so hard to make it work.

"I'll see it when I believe it," is a phrase that cleverly twisted the old chestnut, "I'll believe it when I see it." In fact, changes in belief usually are preceded by changes in reality. Rather than try to create beliefs that are inconsistent with the reality you perceive, change the reality when you can.

Effectiveness and Belief

It's important to understand that you can be an effective creator independent of your belief system. It doesn't matter what you happen to believe. If, however, you try to manipulate your prospect of success by managing the content of your beliefs, you are wasting your time and misdirecting your energies. Not only that, you are setting up an oscillating pattern in which success will eventually be neutralized.

The self-esteem movement has preached that high self-esteem is a prerequisite for a successful life. Millions of taxpayer's dollars have been invested in self-esteem programs in public education throughout the United States and elsewhere. This massive investment was based on the very simple and simplistic idea that if one thinks well of one's self, then he or she will do better, act more productively, feel worthy of success, and so on. How could such an idea generate such traction among a large number of well-meaning and serious people?

The answer is that many people bought the plausibility of the theory. It sounded like a good idea. It seemed like the right idea. But now that time has passed and the funds have been spent, an overwhelming number of studies prove beyond a shadow of doubt that the premise wasn't true. Some of the studies have demonstrated that students with high self-esteem often get into more trouble than those with low self-esteem and that self-esteem "training" has not led to higher student performance.

This should be no surprise to students of history. If we look to the lives of some of the most accomplished people, we find that many of them had what would be defined today as low self-esteem. And yet, they were successful, productive, and able to create what mattered most to them in their lives.

Eliminating Beliefs As A Factor

In our study of structural dynamics, we have seen that the actual content of one's beliefs has no particular impact on one's ability to successfully create the life one wants. But there is a factor that profoundly matters — the *concept* factor.

A belief is a form of concept. Your beliefs about your self could be called self-concepts. Your beliefs about the world could be called world concepts. Your beliefs about the universe could be called philosophic concepts. You may have various personal or social ideals, ideals about children, religion, science, money, sex, relationships, career, politics, and so on. All of these ideals are concepts. They are pictures we may have about the way we think the world should be. They also may include pictures about the ways we think we should be.

In art schools, students learn how to separate concepts from observations. When they draw a still life or a landscape, at first the art students don't actually see what is there. Instead, they often impose a concept on themselves. That is to say, instead of looking at the objects they are drawing, they imagine what it should look like. They have a picture in their head—a concept of what they think they should see. They often paint their concept instead of the actual subject in front of them.

Art teachers train their students to look at reality without the filter of a concept. Art teachers know that concept is the enemy of true observation. They know that students can learn to see reality accurately, but on the road to developing this skill, the person has to restructure his or her focal point.

The study of art illustrates a lesson for us all in learning to apply the creative process to our lives. The most powerful structure we can use to build our lives is structural tension.

What is the difference between an oscillating structure and an advancing structure? CONCEPT.

When I first discovered macrostructural patterns in the early Eighties, I began to experiment with trying to help people change their beliefs. The breakthrough discovery came when we experimented with a *different* notion. Instead of trying to alter the belief, *we eliminate it as part of the structure.*

The belief wasn't changed. It just was no longer an element in the structure. The change of structure led to a change of structural tendencies. If the concept is no longer part of the structure, we only have two elements left: Our desired state and our actual state. In other words, we are left with structural tension, a structure that can resolve and reach equilibrium when we accomplish our goals.

How is that done?

The answer is to see the creative process more accurately. Let's think through why we create. When we create to make a creation, to have something we want to create exist, to bring into being something we care enough about to create, *there is no room for concepts.*

What do your beliefs have to do with the facts that:

- You want something
- You are where you are in current reality, and

- You are willing to take the necessary steps to bring it into being?

Answer — *nothing*. What do you have to believe to want what you want? Who do you have to be? What do you have to think about yourself? Your beliefs are irrelevant to the creative process. So instead of trying to change your beliefs, observe reality more accurately.

Here's reality. You have aspirations. You are where you are now. You will probably have to take a series of actions to get where you want to go. What you think about yourself is irrelevant.

What is relevant is how competent you are, how well you can learn, your ability to observe reality, your ability to focus. These skills can be developed over time. As you create, you will get better at creating.

The point is this: Do not spend any time trying to change your beliefs. Stop the self-manipulation. Instead, think in terms of what you want to create, not who you think you are. The question isn't about you. It's about what you want to create. Also, concepts cloud your ability to see reality more accurately. You need to see reality — the good, the bad, the ugly, the beautiful — as it is. Like the art student, learn the lesson of observing reality without a concept of what you are supposed to be seeing.

You can create more of the life you want, not by manipulating your beliefs, but by learning the skill of creating. Often in life, our aspirations outpace our abilities. When this is the case, the issue is not you or your beliefs but your level of skill. So, by developing your skills, you will eventually be able to accomplish your goals. When your aspirations outpace your abilities, as you engage in the process, there will be moments when you will fail. There will be moments when you look like a blithering idiot. If you made the subject matter "you" rather than "your current ability," you would not be as honest as you need to be when you are bad at something. What is the reason you look so bad? Is it some deep-seated negative belief? Or is it the simple truth that your aspirations are larger than your current ability, and you need to learn how to become competent?

There are many lessons in understanding the phenomenon of macrostructural patterns. Here are some of the most important:

- The events of our lives aren't always what they seem.
- Structure is a dynamic that impacts us profoundly.
- There are two major types of movement that structure generates: oscillating and advancing.
- In an oscillating structure success will eventually be reversed.
- In an advancing structure success can succeed and be built upon.
- Structural Tension is the basic structure for an advancing pattern.
- The concepts we have built into the structure such as questions of self-opinion, social concepts, worldviews form conceptual complexities that create an opposing tension-resolution system to Structural Tension.

One of the great learnings of the past decades since I discovered macrostructural patterns is that we are not doomed to repeat the patterns of the past. We can create a new structure that is capable of real and lasting success. We can build our foundation one building bock at a time, and from that, we can build momentum. The next number of chapters will develop the techniques and principles that help create the best possible design a life can make.

The next chapter explores the way we frame our concepts and the impact that will have in our lives. As we develop these ideas, notice how your own concepts may have been a factor in your personal structural dynamics.

C h a p t e r   1 0

The Conceptual Frame

Certainly, one of the most powerful advantages prehistoric human beings had over their more powerful adversaries in the animal kingdom was imagination. Because we could imagine, we could anticipate what might happen and then either avoid or exploit potential danger. We could imagine how to build traps, which could only be accomplished by understanding the behavioral patterns of other animals. We could invent because we could picture possibilities, processes, the fundamentals of cause and effect, and how the world might react to the action we might take. Because we could think conceptually, we could anticipate the future, discover principles that enabled us to build our communities, heal the sick, educate our children through stories and myths, and develop new ways to live our lives.

But there was something else we did with our ability to conceptualize that wasn't always such a good thing, and that was to create *concepts*.

Concepts Vs Conceptualizing

A concept is a mental model such as ideals, archetypes, and theories about the world. We use our concepts when we don't know how things actually are. You don't need a concept about the color of your eyes, your street address, how old you are, or whether or not you have children. You don't need a concept to realize you are hungry, tired, inspired or entertained.

The word *concept* is a noun. The word *conceptualize* is a verb. A Concept is a *thing*, conceptualizing is an *action*. And not all conceptualizing produces a concept. Rather, conceptualizing often leads to decisions rather than concepts, processes and action plans rather than concepts, experiments rather than concepts, and out-comes rather than concepts.

Conceptualizing is one of the most useful abilities we have when employing the creative process. On the other hand, filling our lives with concepts is one of the most futile activities in which we can engage. The difference between the two is dramatic.

You are conceptualizing when you imagine how the house will look with that new color paint you were thinking about. You are conceptualizing when you imagine what a new job might be like. You are conceptualizing when you picture the alternative route to the airport when traffic is tough and you're twenty minutes behind schedule.

In the beginning stages of the creative process, you are imaging the many possible ways the result may be. This is the period in the cycle when you play with ideas. You are exploring, visualizing, and imaging many possibilities as you consider what you want to create. After that stage in the cycle, you make a choice. From the many possibilities the creation might be, you choose one. You have moved from the conceptual to the vision stage, an evolutionary advance in the cycle. But the advance is made possible by the practice of conceiving various possibilities.

Concepts are forms, constructs, or models about how things are, things like the world, universe, politics, economics, so on, and ourselves.

We use concepts to guide ourselves through our world. They are like roadmaps, policies, rules, warnings, and controls. We feel more able to negotiate the world if we have a concept of how it all works. However, the more we rely on concepts, the less directly we embrace the world. We become less conscious of how reality truly is. We become a bit hypnotized by our concepts. We reexamine the world less and less. Concepts can lead to mindlessness because we assume we know what we might not actually know, we stop questioning and exploring.

Sometimes concepts begin with a real experience. But then, we crystallize the experience into a fixed idea. What was once real becomes artificial as concept replaces inquiry.

As we get older, we often take our experiences and turn them into concepts. As this happens, we live less and less in reality and more and more in our hypnotized mind. We view everything through the distorted lens of our past, and we can't see aspects of reality that contradict our fixed view of the world.

Our Minds and Concepts

Our lives are filled with concepts because our minds generate and adopt them as a dimension of cognition. As we have said, the mind, and structure itself, seeks equilibrium. Another way to express this idea is that your mind wants a resolution to all tensions, a revelation to all mysteries, a solution of all problems, an answer to all questions.

While the mind can perceive reality well, it doesn't care if the resolution it seeks is based on fact or fancy. To the mind, speculation can seem as factual as facts when it is trying to produce equilibrium. Since our minds are inventive, creative, generative, fertile, and so very, very imaginative, they fabricate fiction as easily as non-fiction.

We have to learn to tell the difference between what we actually *observe in* reality, and the concepts we *impose on* reality. If we don't, we may end up in oscillating structures that have profound impact on our ultimate success or failure in reaching our goals. It is critical to understand this insight if we are to create our life as an artist makes a work of art.

Within the tradition of the arts, techniques and processes are drilled into students, teaching them to observe reality rather than be fooled by a concept. In Chapter 5 we heard from art teachers about the dedication and skill it takes to increase the student's level of awareness. Actors, musicians, painters, photographers, and those in similar disciplines must also learn this skill. If they don't, they can never reach the authentic depth of expression they seek. They cannot create structural tension if either of the two factors — vision or current reality — is unclear, and current reality will be unclear if the student is steeped in concepts.

But there is an even more important reason to understand how limiting concepts are and to learn to be fluent in reality. In our work, we have seen absolutely miraculous changes in people's lives when they learn how to separate concept from reality. Old ineffective patterns of behavior that had kept them from reaching what they wanted in life *changed* into new highly effective patterns in which they could achieve their goals, reach a sense of inner freedom and well-being, create overall momentum, and create and experience their lives as an art form.

In the next three chapters, our exploration is to understand the elements of concept that are common in our lives. Next, we see how these various concepts interact with other aspects of our lives and what patterns of behavior the resulting structures produce. Lastly, we will learn to change the underlying structures that take us away from creating the life we want to live.

Conceptual Frames

In the first step, to understand the elements of concept, we frame our concepts in the same way we do the dynamic urge and reality. We have a close up, medium, and a long shot frame of reference.

The Close Up — a concept of danger

The close up view concerns the way we conceptualize fear. Within this frame, we imagine all the things that could go wrong, and we conceive of various negative consequences that might happen.

Fear of negative
consequences

Those who have this concept built into their structures are plagued with apprehension about the future. They often feel a tremendous burden to protect everyone from the perils they think they see. Their fear is not the product of a clear view of the actual danger that exists, but comes from not looking at reality, followed by imaging all the things that could go wrong.

If you were to walk down a dangerous city alley, or engage in risky sports, or walk across a busy eight lane freeway where cars are speeding at eighty miles an hour, you might have a good reason to be afraid. But people who have conceptualized fear always imagine a worse case scenario. Then they react with a high degree of conflict and anxiety. Yet, what they imagine has little to do the actual danger. While conceptual fear is not rooted in reality, to a person in this frame, the concept seems as real as it gets.

Years ago we had a participant attend one of our courses, one that happened to be held in Palm Springs, California. This very nice lady always sat as close to the exit as she could. One day I asked why she did that. "Well," she said, "I live in Nigeria. In Nigeria you could be in a café or a church or a hotel lobby and someone could throw a hand-grenade into the room. So your chances of survival are greater if you sit near the door." As we talked, she told me her husband had died from a grenade being thrown into the restaurant he had been in. He had been sitting in the middle of the room.

The tragedy led this woman to establish a policy of where to sit in a room. She thought that would keep her safe in all situations. But here she was, sitting in one of the more posh resort hotels in one of the most affluent American towns, not Nigeria. Her fear may have been steeped in reality *if* she were in Lagos. But it made no sense in Palm Springs. As the course progressed, and we encouraged her to become more astute and accurate about observing reality as it actually was, she was able to move, little by little, into the room. While changing her seat may sound like a small thing, it turned out to be a tremendous event in her life. Through the process of understanding reality more accurately, she became able to engage more fully in her own life.

This story is a good illustration of what all of us do from time to time. We may have been in a really dangerous situation. Later, we turned that memory into a concept. From then on, when we were in other situations, even ones that were dissimilar, we acted as if we were in the original dangerous one. We confused the second situation with the first, and, as we held a concept of danger, we acted as if the concept was the genuine article.

If you have this close up conceptual frame, you have feelings of concern, risk, or even impending doom, even when there is nothing to stimulate such a feeling in reality. These types of feelings are often about the risk your loved ones may be in. You can imagine the plane crashing, the car getting into an accident, being mugged, or falling out of the ski lift. Why can't they see the danger? If they did see it as well as you do, you could worry less about them.

If you have this concept, you will have trouble trusting others, sometimes their integrity, and always their judgement. And since they don't seem to see the dangers you see, they could be hit by a surprise. How can you trust their judgement if they don't seem to be able to understand how much potential jeopardy there is?

Related to this pattern, when good things happen, you are waiting for the other shoe to fall, because within every silver lining is a dark gray cloud. Your concept is screaming at you, "Look out!"

People who have this conceptual frame often exaggerate danger. Years ago I consulted with a couple who wanted to talk about the disagreement they had in raising their seven-year-old. The father talked about what he saw as the mother's complete lack of responsibility. He proceeded to describe his son riding his big wheel down the steep sidewalk next to their house. "What do you think could happen?" I asked him.

"He could roll out into the street and be hit by a truck!"

I asked the mother what she thought. The first thing she said was that she didn't want to teach her son to have fear in his life. She was directing her remarks more to her husband than to me. In fact, she had developed a compensating strategy, something we see many people do within their relationships. The more fear he expressed, the more she was going to rub his nose in the spirit of a fearless seven-year-old flying down that sidewalk like a bat out of hell.

As we explored reality carefully to see the actual danger that existed, we found out that the mother always checked the street in all directions before the son was permitted to ride his big wheel. She always stood at the end to catch him, a fact she had told her husband every time he raised his fear about the son being hit by a truck. As we tracked reality, I asked him what the *real* danger was given the *actual* situation.

"He could fall off and skin his knee," was what he was left with, not much of a danger after all.

When people with concepts of fear don't have enough evidence to support their fear, they invent pictures of horrible things happening. They need to generate as much conflict as they can so they can put everyone on the alert. There is a big difference between the image of a loved child being run over by a truck and simply falling off a big wheel and bruising his knee. The function of taking a skinned knee and exaggerating it to a life and death matter is typical of people who have a concept of danger as one element in their structural makeup.

(This, along with the other concepts described in this chapter, will be addressed in Chapter 11, so we know how to understand what to do with these types of concepts.)

The Medium Shot – ideals

If we back up from the close up shot to a medium shot, we get three forms of ideals: personal ideals, social ideals, and existential ideals.

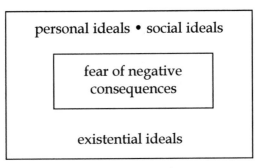

Personal Ideal

A personal ideal is a picture you present to yourself about how you think you should be. The key to understanding this type of ideal is to know that the ideal is not a real desire, but an obligation the person has placed upon him or herself.

This person demands that he or she live up to particular standards. To achieve the ideal can seem like a critical life goal. If the person fails, he or she feels the failure profoundly. But the times when the person succeeds, there is only temporary relief from the inner drive that strives to measure up to the ideal.

Where do these types of personal ideals come from? They come from our unwanted beliefs about ourselves. If a person believes he is a coward, he automatically generates an ideal of being brave. If a person thinks she is stupid, she finds she has an ideal of being smart. If he thinks he is evil, he has an ideal of being good. If she thinks she is nothing special, she has an ideal of being important.

I first wrote about this structure in my book *Creating*. In a chapter entitled *The Ideal-Belief-Reality Conflict* I describe the way that people drive themselves to live up to their ideals so as to hide their unacceptable beliefs from themselves. The last thing they want to have clearly in view is their real opinion of themselves.

Since I wrote *Creating*, we have done years of work on this particular structure and at this point, we know quite a bit about it.

The first thing to understand: Not everyone has this particular structure, yet those who do *always have identity as a major issue in their lives*. Who they are, how they define themselves, how others see them, how they seem to be in various situations, what they can say to themselves about themselves, these are *the* organizing factors of their lives.

They find it hard to separate what they create from their sense of themselves, an essential principle discussed in Chapter 7. To them, everything they do says something about their identity. They look for signals from the environment to tell them how well they're doing. These people may have goals concerning personal development, but these goals are really about getting away from how they really think they are rather than finding their true selves.

In fact, they are afraid to find their true selves, because they suspect what they might find is bad news.

The Boomerang Effect

People do not consciously generate ideals to compensate for their unwanted beliefs. But the ideals they create, nonetheless, do not overcome the belief. As people affirm the ideal, ironically, their affirmations only points back to the unwanted belief. Who, but a person who thought he was a coward, would need to prove he wasn't? Who, but a person who thought she was stupid, would have to prove how clever she was? Who, but a person who thought he was insignificant, would have to prove how significant he was?

The nature of the structure is this: the unwanted belief generates an ideal. The function of the ideal is to obscure the unwanted belief. The person pursues the ideal, and collects many experiences to reinforce it. If the person's unwanted belief is that he is stupid, he may collect degree after degree. Each new doctorate is a symbol of how intelligent he is. But, then,who but a person...? It's the boomerang effect again. The more experiences that are created to argue against the unwanted belief, the more they point back to the unwanted belief. (By the way, this observation should not be misconstrued as implying that all people with many degrees suffer from this structure.)

While this person tries to live up to the ideal, the ideal is sometimes contradicted by reality. We all do stupid things from time to time. When most of us do something stupid, we can laugh at ourselves or at least not suffer an identity crisis. But the person with the ideal of being smart cannot laugh, and he or she does take it personally. To people with an ideal-belief-reality conflict, moments that contradict the ideal are very painful indeed. They often sternly chastise themselves. They put themselves on guard so they will not be guilty of such behavior again. They put pressure on themselves as a form of self-manipulation.

Those with personal ideals often think that others can behave as they want, even their own children. But *they* cannot. They must live up to the ideal they have or their life is a failure. They measure everything by how well they comply to the ideal and avoid the unwanted belief.

The unwanted belief is often invisible to the person. They have spent years hiding it from themselves, collecting experiences that argue against it, affirming the ideal in various ways, and trying to judge themselves by how well they live up to the ideal. But just below the surface is the unwanted belief they have. Occasionally it breaks through the surface, but then it is reburied as fast as possible. However, this personal ideal with its corresponding unwanted belief is the major dynamic in the person's life. It is a force that will dominate until it is understood and dealt with.

Social Ideals

People with social ideals have a very different concept than those with personal ideals. The driving force behind social ideals is that the world is a particular way, and so, everyone should adhere to certain rules and norms.

This was the thought of a man I recently met. He was a real communist. I hadn't met a real one since the Sixties. This fellow had a very clear idea of class distinction with the richer people prone to exploit the poorer people. He measured people by how much money they had, talked about "the working man" as if people who work for a living all agree that they are being unjustly exploited and that a revolution is needed to create economic justice. It was rather interesting to meet such a relic of the past, a bit like meeting a feudalist from the Dark Ages and finding out how such a particular social ideal played in modern times.

This communist fellow had landed in Vermont where he thought he would find kindred spirits — it is the only state in the union that has an honest-to-God socialist representative in Washington. He concluded that a successful socialist politician was a step in the right direction and Vermont was the right place for any self-respecting communist.

The only problem was that Vermont is one place in the world in which class differences barely exist. In Vermont, at town meetings that control the local government, farmers sit with business people sit with school teachers sit with house wives sit with pharmacists sit with plumbers sit with authors sit with game wardens sit with doctors sit with film directors sit with truck drivers. Men and women, young and old, straight and gay, rich and poor, freak and conventional, elitist and Joe-six-pack, somehow all get along with a basic respect for freedom of the individual and, therefore, respect for each other. Not only do they sit together in town meetings, but also they go to community gatherings such as the clambake to raise money for the local volunteer fire fighters or the festive fall fairs held on the village greens every year. They are neighbors and friends and nobody thinks about economic, social, or any other kind of class. This poor communist tried to impose his ideals of the world on anyone who would listen. But they just looked at him with wonder, somewhat puzzled and somewhat amused at yet another eccentric in their midst. He didn't stay in Vermont very long. But he was a walking, breathing, dedicatedly proud owner of one hell of a social ideal.

Many political dogmas give birth to social ideals. The far right has their ideals about how the citizens and government should act in relationship to each other, as does the far left. Political correctness is a social ideal. Many religions have social ideals that they encouragetheir members to follow. The norms within corporations often generate social ideals, so people who join the company soon learn how one should behave while at work.

A friend of mine was exploring his social ideal recently. He talked about often getting enraged by various situations such as someone taking up two parking spaces, some teenagers acting disrespectfully, and a person who spoke to him in a less than friendly way. As we talked about each situation, we found that what made him angry was that these situations were a violation of how he thought people should behave. While most of us would be irritated if someone took two parking spaces, especially if there weren't any others nearby and we wanted to park, our complaint would be about the situation rather than the breaking of a social code. As we talked further, my friend said he saw it as his job to straighten people out who didn't know how they should behave. As we tracked his thinking back to his core concepts, he finally described his view of the world, which was that people needed to create a sense of order for each other, and it was his responsibility to see to it that they knew that.

The only difference between my friend and the communist fellow was the actual content of their social ideal. In both cases, their notion of how the world is was followed by a prescription for behavior that everyone was supposed to follow.

Some people think that if they didn't have the social ideal of a moral or ethical code, people would misbehave.

The assumption built into this notion is that, left to our own devices, we would not make the right choices. We would steal, cheat, lie, swindle, con, defraud people, and commit murder.

It's true that some people do commit these offensive deeds. But for those who do not, is their good behavior a matter of their ethics or morals? Or it is that they have *values* that led them to more constructive behavior? Isn't when we don't have true values when we need a social ideal to follow?

As we have said, values come from determining what is more and what is less important to us. Within the frame of the dynamic urge, values and aspirations fill the medium shot. In the medium shot of the conceptual frame social ideals give us a *concept* of values.

Ethics vs Values

In valueless situations often it is useful to set up rules for fair behavior. Large corporations, as structural entities, are prone to be amoral or valueless. That is to say, while individuals within an organization have values, the business as a whole does not. In light of a valueless system, ethics are better than nothing. At least with ethics the conflict between the members' personal values and the valueless opportunism of the company is reduced. But on a personal level, a concept of values such as moral and ethical codes removes the person from one of his or her deepest dimensions. Just as conceptualized fear is not rooted in the actual danger of a situation, morals and ethics are a conceptualized substitute for one's true values, and are not values themselves.

A few years ago I attended a meeting of a project group. This team worked for one of the world's largest companies. The team was in charge of creating new technology for a product that was to be launched within the next six months. The launch was a gigantic public event with a ten million dollar advertising campaign to catapult it. Big stuff, indeed.

For our illustration of the differences between true values and ethics, I will call this company Macbeth, Inc. People in the company were much more focused on their own position of power within the company than they were on the success of their high-profile product release. Ironically, they began every meeting with a recitation of their "value statement," a list of ethical behaviors they were suppose to adopt. There were about twelve people in the room and there were about twenty-five items on their list. Each member of the team took turns, each read an item until the entire list was read. "We are open." "We are truthful." "We are supportive." "We take risks."And on it went. After the reading of the ethics, the team went to work.

They were hostile to each other, critical, closed, unsupportive, uncivil, difficult, and so on. They even used the list of "values" to criticize each other. "You weren't being open!" someone said to a team member who just raised a legitimate concern about one of the proposed action plans. "You're being unsupportive!" or "You're being risk adverse!" were statements peppered throughout the meeting.

Here was a perfect illustration of the difference between true values and a concept of values. If they actually had the values on the list, they would not have to remind themselves of them at the beginning of every meeting. They *would* operate out of these values. They would have been supportive, truthful, open, etc. To add insult to injury, this group used the list to beat each other up, make each other wrong, power play, and act like a group of spoiled children. The stakes of this particular project were so high for the company, that one wondered if they cared at all about its success.

This is an extreme case, but sometimes by studying the extreme we can see the principle clearly articulated in its more subtle manifestations. Would you rather work for an organization that had good values but didn't have a list of ethics, or an organization that had a list for ethical behavior but didn't have good values? A concept of good behavior assumes that you wouldn't behave well unless you were forced into it. But in the end, concepts can't be a substitute for real values. And trying to impose a social ideal on others never works long term because building a foundation on a concept is like trying to construct a skyscraper on quicksand.

The Existential Ideal

The existential ideal has to do with the notion that the person has to pay for his or her ticket in life. The person with this ideal feels the need to justify his or her existence. Often this person doesn't think the same thing is true for other people. But, this person must do good deeds, accomplish worthy goals, contribute to the earth, and be useful to the world.

Often, this person judges him or herself by how much has been accomplished that day. If enough has been done, one is justified in having a good night sleep. If not enough has been accomplished, the person reviews the day, makes plans for the next day to include greater effort, and feels that he or she hasn't paid sufficiently for life. These people often are very good people who, by their inclinations, values, and aspirations would like to contribute to the world. But their true desires are turned into an ideal in which one has to earn the right to exist.

The Long Shot — mysteries explained

Within our view of reality the long shot frame of reference consists of true mysteries such as where do we come from, is there life after death, where is the universe and what is space, and so on. In the long shot conceptual frame, *mysteries areexplained*. They are explained by philosophic, metaphysical, religious, scientific, or mystical answers.

It has long been the predisposition of humanity to ponder the unanswerable questions and then to supply an answer. But true mysteries are true mysteries because they are in the realm of the unknowable. They are mysteries *because* they can't be understood. Isn't it just like us to try to explain them anyway?

It's fine to speculate about true mysteries as long as we know we are speculating. But many people begin to think that their speculation is more than creating plausible ideas about what might be true. They begin to crystallize their theories into fixed beliefs and worldviews. Then they become "true believers."

We can observe that many people have experiences of God, or The Universe, or Higher Mind, and so on. These experiences can be a source of strength for us. The questions is, what do we do with these experiences? We often transpose them into concepts, and then the concept, rather than the experience, is what is honored.

Can one believe in God and the basic tenants of a formal religion without it being a conceptual frame? *Yes.* This is when one adopts the ideas without transforming them into ideals about the universe. The telltale distinction between the two is how much do you insist upon your point of view being accurate? How much do you try to impose them on others? There is a difference between trying to share your experience with others, and trying to compel others to take on your beliefs.

Others can say, "Here is what I believe, but I could be wrong?" But people in the conceptual frame insist they are right.

Many people want to find the "right" worldview. They think that if they find it, they will know how to act, what direction to go, what meaning their lives should have, and what their assignment is in life. They may read books, go to talks, take courses, study with gurus, attend retreats, and so on. They're on a search for answers to the great mysteries. We can understand the hunger. But the more they fill themselves with concepts the less in touch with life they are.

The extreme version of this is a cult. Every cult has a world-view that demands strict adherence from its members. People are measured by how well they obey. The conceptual realm begins to seem real, and reality can seem like a dream.

In describing the long shot conceptual frame I am not condemning religion or metaphysics. Rather, I am trying to help us separate what is a concept from what is a true mystery. There isn't any conflict between a belief in God and an understanding that there's a lot we don't know about the universe and life that is unknowable from our vantage point as human beings. If anything, faith is the suspension of having to have an answer to the mysteries, rather than insisting upon a concept of Truth.

Concepts

How do concepts figure into our lives? This is the next point of exploration (next chapter.) Our world is so filled with concepts of every sort imaginable that it is no wonder that we can be filled with them. In a world in which concept are seen as a good tool for understanding, we have been encouraged to form them, adopt them, learn them, debate them, make them important, fight over them, and run our lives by them. One only needs to watch a group of television pundits erupt into their nightly shouting match about things of which they know nothing to realize how entrenched the conceptual world has become.

In the arts, concept is the enemy of observation. Concepts blind the artist, dull the writer, reduce the composer and filmmaker to clichés, deaden the actor, and make the poet trite.

But outside of the arts, concepts are often imagined to be a sign of creativity. In a "test" of creativity, the participants sit in a room that has a box placed on a table. They don't know what to expect, but suddenly the box falls open. They are asked to describe what happened. Those who simply describe that the box suddenly fell open are considered less creative than those who speculate about why and how the box came open. Fanciful speculation is considered a higher order thinking skill in some educational circles. But in the arts, the ability to see reality without the filter of a concept, bias, theory, or conjecture is a discipline that takes years to master.

It is easy to fill in the spaces of our understanding with "stuff." Any old stuff will do, with the proviso that it must at least sound plausible. The more plausible, the more theory is taken for fact.

Technically, conceptual sloppiness reduces structural tension because current reality is less well positioned in relationship to the vision we want to create. The bow is unable to generate sufficient tension to propel the arrow toward the goal. And while it may seem very creative to spin fanciful explanations about why a box fell open while you were a test subject for a test on creativity, the reduction of structural tension makes focused invention aimed toward the goal less likely, even as one falls into the trap of free (rather than focused) association.

The major area where the deficit of the conceptual frame shows up is in the structural dynamics of our lives. In the next chapter, we will explore just how our conceptualized fears, ideals, and worldviews can lead to oscillating patterns that reverse our successes and neutralize our advances.

The Structures of Our Lives

The structures in our lives will determine to a large degree our life journey. What are these structures? They consist of the relationships among elements such as our aspirations, our abilities, our talents, the conditions we are in, our concepts and beliefs, and our values. One structure we have been describing throughout this book as a fundamental to the creative process and, therefore, to building your life is structural tension. As we have developed this theme, we have seen that the structure that is most capable of leading to successful outcomes, and building on that success comes from true aspirations and values, and a clear sense of the overall shapes and patterns of current reality. Medium shots for both the dynamic urge and actual frames are the strongest arrangement of these elements.

But often there is another element built into the structure. This is when the conceptual frame that we explored in the last chapter plays a role in the final success or failure of our creative process.

The Causal Set

When elements combine, they create a single unit of structure. Each element is an individual force. But the sum is more than a collection of individual forces. They impact each other. Remember our example from the film *Casablanca*? Rick, Ilsa, and Victor together formed a structural unit. They had their own goals within the plot, but each of their goals was tied to the other characters. This is how it is in the structure we are about to explore. Within this structure there are three distinct forces that, while they exist separately, profoundly impact each other. We call this unit of structure the *causal set*.

The causal set consists of a combination of the *dynamic urge*, and the *conceptual* and *actual* frames.

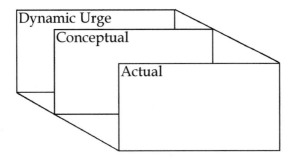

Below is an example of a typical causal set in which the person's dynamic urge is focused on aspirations (she has true desires for accomplishment); the conceptual frame is focused on fear of imaginary negative consequences (she imagines that success brings danger); and she sees reality from the perspective of overall shapes and patterns (she has a sense of a longer time frame in which she can see how past events lead to future consequences).

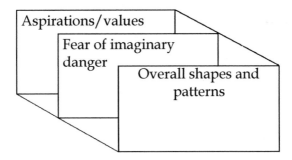

Let's illustrate the above structure with more detail to better understand how the causal set works: The person in question wants to build a new business; and she can understand the business environment she is in, and can see the trends, the challenges, the opportunities, and her own personal talents and skills. But also, she has a subconscious fear that success can be dangerous and if she is too successful, something bad will happen to her.

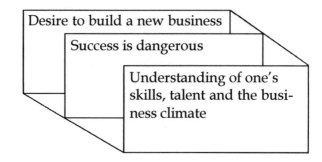

A structure like the one above will lead predictably to an oscillating pattern. To understand the actual dynamics, let's put together two fundamental laws about structure:

- Tension seeks resolution
- Structure seeks equilibrium

As we have said, tension is caused by a contrast or difference between or among elements of a structure. Some elements pull in one direction, some in the opposite directions. In the above example, there is more than one relationship that the structure must address.

One relationship is the tension between the dynamic urge and the actual situation. She wants to build a new business, and she understands her starting point.

In the beginning, this tension will be the most pronounced, and so the structure will give rise to behaviors that support her goal of building a successful business.

But as she moves closer and closer toward that goal, a shift occurs. The concept of danger or impending doom begins to play a bigger and bigger role in the structure, especially as she achieves more and more success. The bigger tension is now the relationship between the successful outcome and her growing sense of danger.

This person may not know why she begins to feel trepidation, especially in light of how well things are going. She may call it an intuition or a hunch or some unspoken dread that she experiences about the business she is creating.

The new major tension seeks its own resolution. This is because tension seeks resolution, and the causal set seeks equilibrium. The structure's goal is not our subject's goal. She wants a successful business. The structure wants to produce equilibrium—the degree of tension in both systems is exactly the same.

Let's illustrate this example with our rubber band metaphor. Our subject is standing in a room. She has a rubber band tied from her waist to one of the walls. She has a second rubber band tied from her waist to the other wall. These are two competing tension-resolution systems.

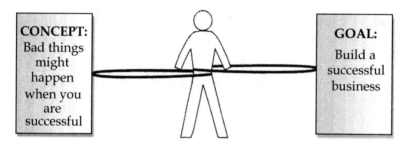

As she begins to move toward her goal, the rubber band in front of her relaxes its tension, but the one in back becomes more tense. It now becomes easier for her to move away from her goal because the structure wants to resolve the bigger tension that now dominates the system.

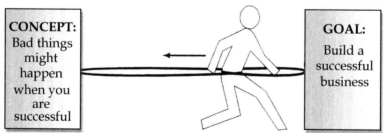

Once our lady begins to move away from the success she has created, the tension moving her away begins to resolve.

Once the reversal has reduced the tension in the concept system, she feels the emerging new surge of desire. Our subject may get an idea for a new business venture. A new shift of dominance takes place, and she is about to repeat the same pattern again.

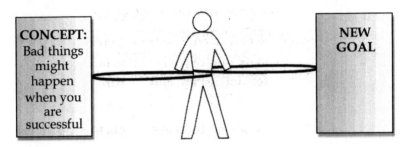

Each individual has a different pattern in his or her "story line" as to how a success is reversed. Some people become bored, others create a crisis. Some people find other interests that distract them, and some people have a run of "bad luck." The point is less about the typical event that happens, than about why it happens. In this structure, success will inevitably be reversed.

This does not mean that people are doomed by their structures. The principle is, however, that you can't get where you want to go and build upon that success from within this structure. Success will always be reversed within this structure, and so, "You can't get there from here."

First, you need to go somewhere else. The somewhere else is a different structure. A change of the underlying structures in your life will dramatically change your prospects of full, non-reversible success. We develop this idea in the next chapter.

In this structure, equilibrium is impossible to achieve. But the structure will try to achieve it anyway. It will react to the most pronounced tension. As it moves toward a resolution of that tension, other tensions will then become dominant, and the structure will begin to work to reduce them. The state of non-equilibrium will create an impetus for action—action that is designed to reduce the prevailing tension of the moment.

The equilibrium cycle

The causal set contains shifting degrees of non-equilibrium. Each major tension leads to actions to reduce the tension. As the actions do, in fact, change the state of tension, and as new tensions become dominant, a new condition of non-equilibrium demands attention. This sets up a very dynamic cycle of oscillation. The causal set launches a feedback system.

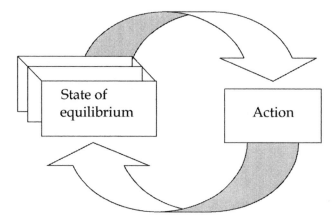

Each time the cycle generates an action, it alters one of the tension-resolution systems. This changes the nature of the state of equilibrium, which leads to yet another action, and so on.

Another Causal Set

Let's take a look at other possible causal sets. In this next one, the person has vague hopes on the level of the dynamic urge (long shot), he has a personal ideal in the conceptual frame (medium shot), and he views reality in obsessive details (close up).

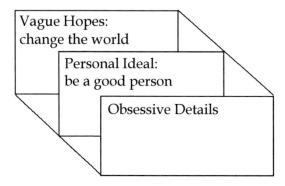

Let's say this person wants to change the world for the better; just how is unclear; the vision is too vague to organize around. It is not that the person is insincere but rather that he doesn't know much about what he actually wants to create.

Let's add to the picture that he thinks he is a bad person; this is his concept. To compensate for this belief, he has formed an ideal of himself as a good person. This ideal includes the notion that a good person is dedicated to helping the world, contending with the "big issues," and being seen as an important force for good in the world.

Let's further add to this structure his habit of viewing reality in very short time frames, many many details, and not a lot of context for these details. In a discussion with him, we might find him describing detailed statistics about world population, water availability, pollution, and technology, but the details do not lead to an understanding of trends.

Given these factors, what might the structure produce? The structure's major tension is between this person's ideal to be seen as a good person in contrast with the reality in which there are overwhelming details with which to contend. The vague hope that he could help change the world isn't defined enough to create an adequate tension between his desired state and his actual state.

In this structure, the person lives quite a bit in his head. Lots of wheel-spinning gives him the impression that he is doing a lot. Sifting through the minutia of details is a lot of work even though it doesn't lead too much real action.

This person experiences considerable frustration. He feels he is working very hard on important issues but is ineffective. Frustration can lead to anger, and he will then react against what seems to be the world's indifference to an important cause. He may also become cynical over time. His state of powerlessness, his focus on identity, his inability to see the overall shapes and patterns in reality make it hard for him to see his own hand in what his life has become.

This person thinks a lot about his place in the world. In a sense, that is the major tension in the structure—one that is never resolved. His hidden belief—he is a bad person— cannot be disclosed to anyone, especially himself. Self-reflection will simply lead to obsessing about details, and tying his hopes for a better world on proving that he is a good person.

As with all of these structures, a change of structure will lead to true transformation. This person can have a rebirth into his own life-building process. Yet, without a change of the underlying structures, he will repeat his current experience again and again.

The Bill Clinton Causal Set

There are twenty-seven types of causal sets. Each has a dynamic urge, a conceptual frame, and a reality frame. Beyond that, many people's structure changes from one causal set to another as the cycle continues its feedback in search of final equilibrium.

In one iteration of the cycle, the person may have a clear view of overall shapes and patterns in her view of reality. But later, the person becomes obsessively detailed. A person may be focused on aspirations and values, but later in the cycle his focus changes to instincts and appetites. There are many examples of this last shift in public life in which a person in an important position does something terribly stupid, something which leads to a massive scandal. Many wondered how someone as intelligent and politically savvy as Bill Clinton could jeopardize his career and legacy as president by having a frivolous affair with an intern. Pundits and his enemies talked about his arrogance, his smugness, and his disdain for proper ethics. A structural look at the same events gives us a very different understanding of the dynamics involved.

If he had a shift in his dynamic urge from aspirations and values to appetites and instincts, one of the experiential changes is how time passes. In the medium shot, time is phrased in longer periods. One sees how the past connects with the present and connects with the future. But in the close up view of appetites, time is experienced in the moment. A sense of past and future are almost non-existent. Sometimes we talk of a person's reptilian brain taking over, and he or she reacts the same way a snake or a frog might react.

Well, in Clinton's case, it was his teenage brain that took over. Suddenly he wasn't thinking like the most powerful man in the world. Instead, he was thinking like a seventeen-year-old boy in the back of his family's car, parking with a girl on lover's lane. It wasn't a matter of how smart he was, how arrogant he might be, or any of the other explanations people have attributed to him. He was in an oscillating structure in which his success would be reversed. This type of scandal was predicted years before by David

Maraniss in his excellent biography about Clinton *First In His Class: A Biography of Bill Clinton.* Many good biographers can see their subject's patterns, and Maraniss was very astute in naming the type of reversal that Clinton would have well before he had it.

Clinton's public support during this scandal was a total surprise to the pundits who thought he would be jeered out of office in a matter of weeks. But the public seems to have more wisdom than the pundits and kept his approval rating in the stratosphere. This was also part of his pattern.

How to Change The Structure From Oscillating to Advancing

A change of underlying structure happens when we change the elements within the structure. If the causal set is attempting to produce equilibrium within a combination of dynamic urge, conceptual, and the actual, eliminating one of these factors will change the structural tendencies. If, for example, you didn't want to create anything and had no desire at all, there wouldn't be a tension between your concepts and reality. You could fear conceptual danger given that you weren't trying to accomplish anything, you could stay home and focus on keeping yourself safe.

But, since we have true desires and want to create, this is a very unworkable strategy.

We could attempt to give up our understanding of reality. If we could do that, we could have as many fictitious concepts as we liked, but what difference would it make? We wouldn't know if we were accomplishing our goals or not, because reality would not be understood. Most of us would find this an unworkable strategy because we have been cursed with sanity.

But, if we eliminate our concepts, what are we left with?

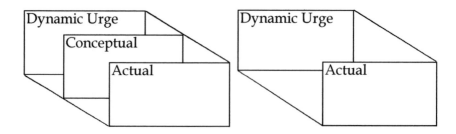

THAT'S RIGHT! STRUCTURAL TENSION!

Let's say this technically for a moment. If we move from a causal set that has three elements that cannot achieve a state of final equilibrium to a causal set that has only two elements that can achieve final equilibrium, we have moved from an oscillating structure to a resolving or advancing structure.

To make this shift, one needs to eliminate his or her concepts. We will explore just how to do that in the next chapter, but let's end this chapter with the punch line that can change your life:

- Understand what you want to create
- Know reality
- Establish structural tension
- Eliminate the concepts you have built into your life

When you do this, you will be in a position to create much of what you want in your life. You will be able to build on your successes, learn from your mistakes, and advance through your life from creation to creation. You will be able to live in the orientation of the artist, focused on the creative act, involved with the truest spirit of your life, generative, alive, and in touch with what is highest and deepest in you.

A Concept-Free Structure

N ot all concepts are addressed in the same way. In this chapter we will show you how to eliminate the major concepts people have built within the causal set, the concepts discussed in Chapter 10. The major purpose of this chapter is to enable you to free yourself from the prevailing concepts that may be causing oscillation in your life, and to redesign your life structures so that they advance.

The best way to work with this material is to understand the general ideas and then to experiment with the principles that are discussed.

Fear of imaginary danger

The close up view of in the conceptual frame is a fear that negative consequences may befall you or your loved ones because there is danger lurking in life's various situations. Others seem to be unaware of the potential danger, so you feel a special responsibility to alert your loved ones and protect them.

To a person with fear of imaginary danger, the unknown is assumed to be perilous. The person is always on-guard, and trying to avert disaster. They always assume a worst-case scenario. If you have this structure, your imagination is working overtime.

If you have this structure, you will find that your tendency is to try to control the conditions that seem threatening. You will develop a control strategy that won't quit.

The control strategy

The most endearing thing about people in this structure is that they are good-hearted folks who want to protect their loved ones from misfortune. They cannot understand why the people on the other side of their control strategy resist their attempts to protect them. Ironically, the control strategy is not about power-wielding, domination, or authority. Rather, it is about safety and protection. Control people feel threatened constantly, although sometimes it is at a low volume. The control strategy tightens when the volume becomes high. If this is your structure, you will limit the input from others, especially if they argue against your claims of danger. You will cut them off, not let them finish their sentences, or shout them down. You may stop them from expressing their point of view by getting upset, threatening to leave the room, or taking on the look of a hurt child who has just been told bad news about his dog. Another thing you may do is avoid reading articles or seeing newscasts that suggest that the situation is less dangerous than you imagine.

A value conflict

People with a control strategy often are in conflict with their innate value of freedom. On the one hand, they think that people are free to live their lives the way each individual sees fit. On the other hand, they want to protect them against danger.

All value conflicts are resolved by establishing a hierarchy. Which value is more important? Often, when the question of values are brought into the picture, a person with a control strategy will choose freedom over control. This new focus enables the person to give up control in favor of supporting others in living their own lives.

How much control do we have?

We are creative beings, predisposed to create our lives whenever we can. But there are so many aspects of our lives we do not control, such as our life span, the fate of our loved ones, the random nature of freak accidents that can happen. To the control person, this is not a welcomed insight. But if they are to be fluent in reality, they must come to understand this fact:

You can't control what you can't control.

Where we don't have the possibility of control, we must stop *trying* to control. There might be actual danger in our lives, but if it is in the realm of the uncontrollable, we cannot protect others or ourselves from it. It is human to think we can. It is also human to rethink our situation, come to terms with reality exactly as it is, and, from that understanding, do the best we can.

An old *Twilight Zone* TV program really illustrated this point. A man kept having a reoccurring dream in which a plane crashed into his house. Each night he would have the same dream, each time with more and more detail. After a while, he knew the date of the plane crash, the time, and even the serial number on the plane. As the plot developed, he called the airport and found that this number was real. He tracked down the plane's owner and tried to warn him not to fly on the datehe had dreamed about. The owner thought he was crazy and sent him away. The fateful night came, and the man decided to leave his home and move to a motel to stay out of harm's way. But, just at the hour he had dreamed, the plane came crashing into his motel room.

Even though *The Twilight Zone* was a classic of the ironic and fanciful, it often had a wonderful twist of truth to it. This episode could have been called, *You Can't Control What You Can't Control*.

How to work with imaginary danger

Reality includes two factors that address imagined danger:

- The actual level of danger that really exists
- The inability to control what we can't control

If you find that you have this concept, there is only one place to go, and that's *reality*. What is the *actual* danger? How do you know? What can you *actually* do in light of the unknown?

Do not assume that the danger you imagine is real. Check the real potential for danger, rather than simply imagining a worst case scenario, a scenario you may be inventing. You need to shift your process from imagination to observation. Look rather than assume.

Even though you study reality more precisely, you may still feel stress and anxiety. Since the trepidation you feel is generated by your *concept*, don't think your apprehension is a warning from your intuition, sixth sense, or psychic perception. Rather than coming from these human abilities we all have, it simply comes from your emotional reactive patterns. Over time, these emotional reactive patterns will change, and, because you are increasing your awareness of reality, they will disappear.

Realize the futility of trying to control circumstances when you actually have no control. At worse, it is destructive to your health. It increases your level of stress, increases your experience of powerlessness, and produces chronic frustration.

If you stop trying to control what you can't control, and begin to evaluate reality's danger accurately, you will have a profound change of underlying structure. You will move from chronic oscillation to a pattern of achievement, involvement, and a heightened ability to create.

The Personal Ideal

Many people have created ideals for themselves. But, too often, the ideal is only a compensation for an unwanted belief.

The function of the ideal is to offset the belief and hide it. Because of this, the most unacceptable beliefs we may have about ourselves are often invisible. If you are in this structure, you can do a little detective work to discover what your unwanted belief is. You can then work with this belief within the context of structural dynamics.

Your life will be filled with two types of experiences: ones in which you live up to your ideal and ones in which you fail. Both experiences can provide us with clues. Here are some thought experiments that can help.

> • Remember a time in which you succeeded, and then ask yourself why you were so pleased.

Certainly it is good to accomplish sought-after goals. But, if you have a personal ideal, your pleasure is not as much about the accomplishment itself, but rather how well you performed. You focus on your identity and what the success seems to say about you.

Focusing on identity during times of success is a two-sided coin. Sometimes, what's seems more important than the positive affirmation of the ideal, is what the success seems to deny or argue against. Does it prove you are not what you are afraid you might be? If you were especially brilliant in this case, does that argue you are not stupid? If you were especially useful, does it argue you are not useless? If you were especially brave, does it argue you are not a coward?

- Remember a time when you failed to live up to your ideal, and then ask yourself what you told yourself.

If you had a personal ideal, you took it very personally indeed. Each event was being followed by intense self-criticism and self-censure. Your friends may advise you not to be so hard on yourself. Too bad you find it impossible to take their advice.

Why are you so hard on yourself? You are trying to prevent yourself from failing in the future. Failure points to your hidden belief. In essence, you are saying, "I better not be what I'm afraid I am."

Throughout, your focus will be on identity. Who are you, what are you, how do you see yourself, and how do others see you?

You may find yourself thinking, "What kind of person acts the way I did? Why do I have to be such a loser? Can't I ever learn to get it right? What's wrong with me?"

How to work with this structure

In our work on structural dynamics, we have discovered the best way to work with this structure is radically different from the pop-psychology standards of today. First we help the person discover his or her hidden belief. Next, we look at the role it plays in the major events of his or her life.

One major difference in our work is that we do not try to help the person change the belief, or create higher self-esteem, or affirm positive statements, or argue that the belief is groundless given the successful life-experiences the person has had.

As discussed previously, these methods, while popular, do not enable people to accomplish a true change of their structure. These techniques only widen the magnitude of the oscillating pattern the person is in. Yes, when these methods are used, at first things will be better, because at least some of the time an oscillating pattern moves toward your goal. But there will be a reversal, and eventually things will get worse than before.

In working with an individual who has a personal ideal, if the person is self-critical of having made a mistake, we might ask, "Why does it matter that you made a mistake?" There are many ways this question can be answered. But the person within an ideal-belief-reality conflict will track it to how it makes him or her "look."

A typical series of questions and answers might be:

> "Why does it matter that you made a mistake?"
> "Because I'm not the kind of person who makes that kind of mistake."
> "What kind of person does make that kind of mistake?"
> "A stupid person."

In this example, perhaps our client thinks he or she is stupid. Most of us have been trained to think that it's not okay to have a negative self-opinion. Therefore, most of us would try to change our mind, arguing that just making a mistake doesn't mean we're stupid. We might point to all the clever things we have done. We might point to all the stupid little mistakes Einstein made in his life.

People with an ideal-belief-reality conflict want desperately to be convinced. The last thing in the world they want is to think that they're stupid. So the person will try to accept our argument.

But, our best efforts do not help. Trying to change the unwanted belief boomerangs. Who, but a person who thought he or she was stupid, would try to prove to it wasn't so?

What would motivate a change of belief?

Trying to change an unacceptable belief leads back to the belief itself.

Of course, people change many of their ideas about themselves throughout their lives. If they can't drive, and then they learn to drive, they may change their belief about driving. These types of changes of belief are, however, not identity related. They are factually based.

But beliefs about self-opinion are not based on reality. There is no accurate way to define someone. Who has the absolute authority to determine what a person is?

We may regard the person who thinks she is useless as a very useful member of society. We may consider the person who thinks he is bad is a very good person. We may believe that the person who thinks she is unimportant is very important. But, at the end of the day, our opinion doesn't count.

Affirmations: an exercise in futility

The practice of trying to affirm a positive belief to replace the negative belief is another exercise in futility.

Often people try to use affirmations to program the subconscious mind. The hope is that the subconscious will learn to manifest experiences that are consistent with the suggestions it is given. But, the subconscious also understands the motivation for the affirmation. We do not spend time affirming those things we think are true. We do not affirm our street address, the color of our eyes, how many children we have, or how tall we are. We only affirm things that are in question, i.e., things we do not think are really true.

The usual method begins with a relaxation technique, followed by repeating a statement such as, "I am a person who is loving, whole, useful, and courageous." While the hope is that the mind will learn the new program and act accordingly, what actually happens is that the mind understands there is an important and influential belief that must be stopped. The motivation for the affirmation boomerangs and reinforces two things: The unwanted belief is true, and the belief is powerful. "I am a person who is loving, whole, useful, and courageous," translates to, "I am unloving, fragmented, useless, and a coward."

The best approach

In working with this structure, we have found the very best approach is to first discover the actual belief, then to see how it impacts the person's life, and then to eliminate it as a factor in the structure.

Let's say that the person believes she is unimportant. We then look at how the belief shows up in the events of her life.

We may see that she often tries to know important people, but she does so hoping that some of their importance will rub off, therefore arguing against her belief.

She may try to accomplish what seem to be important goals. When we track her thinking about this, we may find that she is more focused on what such goals seem to say about her rather than her interest in the goals themselves. She may become a world expert in important issues and be very accomplished in her field. But, as we track her thinking, we will find that she is compensating for her belief that she is unimportant.

Compensating strategies like these are very common. When we track the person's internal motivations, the avoidance of the unwanted belief becomes exceedingly transparent.

Knowing the Belief

People in this structure can come to understand they have a belief that they find unacceptable. And they can see the central role this belief has played in their lives. Rather than trying to change the belief, we work with this belief in two steps.

Step one is to know the belief or, in our terms, become fluent in the belief.

For example, if a person thinks he is stupid, he can get to know his own belief better. He can begin by studying his life. Why has he done some of the things he has?

At first, the person can see all the ways he has tried to prove he was smart. He can remember recent episodes in which he was up to his old tricks, trying to offset anyone thinking he was stupid and trying to get them to think he was smart. He also will begin to rethink some of the major events of his life when he was compensating for his belief. This may include goals he pursued and achievements he sought. For example, the times he tried to be clever so everyone would know how smart he was or the degrees and credentials he collected to show how smart he is or the clever wisecracks he makes to be seen as being clever or the wealth of information he has at his fingertips to prove he isn't stupid.

We must remember that the person's compensating strategy is to hide the belief. So, as the belief becomes obvious, the person experiences growing conflict. The clearer the belief, the more anxiety experienced. Over time, this experience will change, and the emotional charge the person feels at the beginning of the exploration will disappear.

In Denial

In the next phase, as the true belief becomes clear, the person tries to deny it. He may simply minimize the importance of the belief by quick agreement. "Yes, I think I'm stupid. I got it. Let's not talk about this anymore." At this point, there isn't a change of underlying structure. Instead, the person is just reacting to the emotional conflict he feels. He wants this sudden realization to all go away so he will feel better.

But feeling better is in conflict with pursing reality and truth. In this case, there is no way to determine the truth of the belief itself, since all we have in the realm of self-opinion is opinion, not fact. So, reality is not about whether the person is really stupid, useless, or a loser, etc. Rather, reality is that the person *thinks* the belief is accurate.

In fact, the more the person tries to avoid knowing his or her own opinion, the more important it is in the structure. Trying to change it makes the belief seem terribly important. Trying to prove it wrong does the same thing. Trying to show how experiences to the contrary argue against the belief make the unwanted belief seem critically important.

Often, the person reaches a point where there is a choice between two conflicting interests: reducing the emotional discomfort or seeing what is really going on.

The person needs to make a value choice at this point.

"Which is more important to you, seeing reality or feeling okay?"

Almost always, the person chooses to see reality, and therefore, to let the emotional chips fall wherever they may.

After this, the person can more easily look at reality. He or she is able to see the patterns and overall shapes that exist. These people begin to understand exactly how much they have hated this thought they have about themselves and how much it has been a factor in their lives.

As we work together, the person comes to know what is believed about him or herself. At a certain point of this exploration, a strange thing happens. The person's belief doesn't change, but all of the emotional charge the person has placed on the unwanted belief vanishes. Previously, the person's attempt to hide the belief from him or herself generates an elaborate compensating strategy. But, once the cat is out of the bag, there is no reason to hide the belief from anyone. In essence, the concept is no longer an element of the causal set. How they are, who they are, what they are, these become irrelevant questions to their creative process.

People who have gone through this thought process find an almost instant change in their lives. Suddenly, they can be much more effective, more able to learn, more able to enjoy life, more focused on their real aspirations, values, and reality.

This is not to say that people then like what they believe about themselves. They don't. But how smart, good, important, useful, worthy, etc is not a factor in their lives. If anything, there is often a new ironic pleasure they discover. To the person who thinks he is stupid, now he can say, "Boy, for a guy who is stupid, I've done pretty well."

A change of underlying structure that occurs from this exploration is a truly profound transformation. Life becomes filled with new possibilities, new probabilities, and a new lease on life.

Social Ideals

If you have social ideals, you can work with these by putting your *values* before your *concepts*. The question that always helps is this: Are people free to try to live their lives the way they want?

Thinking about freedom is often made difficult when we confuse freedom with sovereignty. The following statement illustrates this confusion: "People aren't free to throw their garbage on my lawn." Throwing garbage on lawns is not about freedom. It is a sovereignty issue. Sovereignty concerns ownership and authority. When it's *my* lawn, I have the authority to determine who gets to do what on it. Without my consent, no one else has the privilege to make decisions about it.

Sovereignty issues cloud the deeper questions about the value of freedom. Do we think that individuals have the right to live their lives the ways they want? If not, why not? If someone decides to try to become a great sculptor, even if she has limited talent, is she free to organize her life to pursue her aim? And furthermore, should she be free to do so, even if she has only a modest chance for success?

Most people answer yes. And that's the point. When we try to make rules for people and then coerce them to live up to our rules, we assume they do not have the right to freely live their lives their way. What gives us the authority to make up the rules for others?

Those with social ideals often distort reality when facts argue against their ideal. The ideal becomes the standard against which reality and aspirations are measured. So, often the concept obscures a person's true aspirations. When this concept is eliminated from the system, your true desires can become clear. Reality can be seen objectively. And as we noted in the last chapter, when you eliminate the concept from the structure, the new structure is structural tension. It can now become the dominant force in your life. You are ready to create the life you want to create.

Existential Ideals

If you have this concept, you will feel that you must justify your existence. The question that can help you see the folly of this is: "How does what you do justify your existence?" Can anything justify your right to exist? How can it?

The fact is that you exist. The fact is that there isn't a real justification for our lives. We may want to help people, serve the community, invent new drugs that treat illness, invent new technology, etc. But these aspirations may be your true desire anyway and, therefore, not have the ulterior motive of trying to justify your existence.

Even if you wanted to justify your existence, you can't. This fact will free you from the existential ideal you may have.

You may need to rethink this question over a short period to have it penetrate more deeply into your awareness. If so, ask the same questions again. Answering them will bring you to the point where concept is eliminated and structural tension is in place in your life.

Mysteries Explained

The person who has this concept often looks for unifying theories that tie all the threads in life together. But, true mysteries are in the realm of the unknowable. Rather that search for understanding, you can understand that concepts do not give answers to life's mysteries. Therefore, suspend the questions and let the mysteries be mysteries.

A Life Without Concepts

How would you spend your time if you didn't have to avoid conceptual danger, live up to an ideal, adhere to various rules, justify your existence, or understand the great mysteries in life? Probable answer: Any way you want.

When concepts are no longer a factor in your creative process, you can focus on what you do want. You don't have to be a particular way to create your goals. You don't have to understand the rules or the world. You can be involved with your life in the most wondrous of ways. Not only that the structures in your life will begin to support your creative process. Your life will become an art that develops, builds, and grows.

The most profound advice I can give you, advice that will change your life for the better: *Eradicate concepts from your life.*

Free yourself from them, and you will experience true freedom. Your life patterns will advance, and you will be able to build on your successes and even on your failures. You will internalize structural tension so that your mind will be focused on your next creations, the current reality involved, and the strategies you might employ to accomplish your goals.

The act of creating occurs in reality, and the more we can live in reality, the more we touch the deeper essence of the creative process and ourselves. Then, more and more, our life becomes the work of art we want to create.

Artistry in Action

Vehicles For Your Life

T he rock star and international phenomenon Madonna virtually invented reinventing herself. Just when her public thought they had a fix on her, she would change. When she did, she created a new type of Madonna, a Madonna with a different hairstyle and color, different type of wardrobe, different musical style, different persona, and different content of her music. She so easily moved from punky rocker to the material girl to the dark-haired lady of mystery to a cowgirl to so many other characters. But all the while, she was still the real Madonna, and each vehicle she created was the right platform for her art.

This short chapter is about creating vehicles for expression in life. Think of a vehicle as a container in which you can travel. Just as a car is a vehicle, your body is a vehicle. Your personality is another type of vehicle. Your clothing style is another vehicle. We often develop various vehicles to negotiate our world.

Our Many Vehicles

Most of us use four or five major vehicles such as the parent vehicle, the professional vehicle, the friend, family member, community leader, son or daughter vehicle.

At work we may dress a certain way, speak a certain way, and use social customs and manners that are appropriate to our professional world. But when we go home we may change our clothes, our speech patterns, our manners, our personalities.

If we begin to define and create the various vehicles we use more consciously, we will more effectively move through our life.

Before we engage in creating a number of suitable vehicles for our life we must understand that each vehicle is a true expression of ourselves. We are not creating phony characters in an attempt to con the people in our life. We are not being inauthentic simply because we have many ways of being. We are simply doing what we do anyway, but doing it better.

What will be consistent with each vehicle you create for yourself are your values and your aspirations. Also your talents, intelligence, sensibilities, personal rhythms, and so on, will always be there. When you create a vehicle you are not pretending to be someone else. Rather, you are broadening the range of possible ways you actually are. There are many dimensions to you, and different vehicles require different aspects of yourself.

Many people have a special vehicle when they travel. They know when to get to the airport, when to check in, where to buy magazines, when to board the plane, what to eat or drink on board, and so on. Beyond that, they have a particular way of being when they travel alone. They may have another vehicle when they travel with their families. We may have another vehicle when we go to the gym to exercise, another one when we apply for a loan at the bank. We can better develop our vehicles consciously, and this helps us better create our life.

Mapping Your Vehicles

Take out a piece of paper and write down the current vehicles you use now. You may need to do a little thinking about this. There will be the obvious ones that immediately come to mind. When I have done this with workshop participants, they always have some that relate to work, some that are from the relationships in their lives, some that have to do with their interests, etc. But, these people make new discoveries. One woman saw that she was a major leader in her field. Before the exercise, she had avoided the idea. But, in fact, her professional success had put her in that position. Her tendency was to ignore her leadership role because she didn't seek it and was reluctant to see herself as powerful. Once, however, she saw that she did have that role, she constructed a vehicle to better lead. She designed what she needed as a leader: the skills, focus, temperament, and art. This exercise helped her separate herself from her role, and, therefore, she could develop her ability to lead more effectively.

Another person discovered that he likes to be a deal maker. He never thought about this before, but he did love making real-estate deals, merchandising deals, business deals,and contract deals. He decided to perfect his deal-making vehicle.

The characteristic of each vehicle you create is it has your touch in them no matter how varied it is. It's still you having fun at the skating rink, at the board meeting, at the theater, meeting with your child's teacher, buying groceries, mowing your lawn, managing the product team, having a romantic dinner, or playing bridge.

So, write down the most important vehicles you use in your life.

Creating a Better Vehicle

Next, for each vehicle, write a list of the skills or attributes that would help you create a better vehicle. These skills may include abilities you may want to develop, facilities you want to acquire, talents you want to improve, or aptitudes you want to enlarge. Note anything else that might seem useful in developing these vehicles.

Do this now.

Practice, Practice, Practice

Finally, practice developing each of the vehicles when you are using them. This will make you more and more effective, but, even more importantly, it will enable you to see some of the ways you are a creator in your life. You are the creator of the vehicles which, in turn, are used to better create the aims you are after.

C h a p t e r   1 4

Your Life as a Learner

One commonality artists have is their devotion to learning: there is always something to discover, master, develop, find, reach and see. Learning is an orientation built into a way of being. When you are in a learning mode, you do not assume you know everything. You assume you don't know enough. The tension between what is known and what is not known is a structural dynamic that leads us forward.

If the creative process is anything, it's a learning process. In creating your life as art, one thing you must become is a learner.

A Way of Life

Learning is a way of life. And while many people like learning for the shear joy of it, the most difficult aspects of learning are often not fun. It's easy to learn when it's entertaining, recreational, and engaging. It's not so easy when you must confront embarrassment, discomfort, and distress.

If you love to learn how to cook a new cuisine, how to grow organic vegetables, how to sail, how to snowboard, this type of learning is most often a pleasure. Two things motivate you: your interest in the activity, and your delight during the process of learning.

But there is another type of learning, one that is not always so welcomed: the learning that life forces upon us. Hardships, disappointments, failures, and misfortune can be hard teachers indeed. And yet, often, we learn most from adversity.

Going through bad times forces us to dig deeper into ourselves, review some of our most basic premises, rethink our values, and find our own source of inner strength.

People who have survived accidents often say things like, "While it was terrible, it was one of the best things that ever happened to me." They say this because they were forced to confront aspects of themselves they would not have without the accident.

Sometimes a failed love affair forces you to rethink your values of personal freedom. You may have wanted someone you loved to love you back, but they didn't. What did you do? You may have tried various forms of manipulation, from charm to the hurt puppy approach. You may have sent flowers one day and threatened to live your life as a celibate monk the next, but nothing worked. Banging your head against the wall may have finally knocked some sense into you as you were forced to re-examine your values. Many people point to an unrequited love experience as a great teacher in helping them reach maturity and tolerance.

The other day I heard a retired pilot talk about his experience of being fired from his job. He had become an alcoholic, and he had been flying the plane under the influence. After being fired, he resented the company for taking this action. But it forced him to take an honest look at himself and what he had become.

Moments like these are often the catalyst for profound transformation. In this case, he began to discover what truly mattered to him. He gave up drinking, found his own source of inner strength, cleaned up his act, slowly built his career back up, and years later was rehired by the company that had fired him. He worked there many years before retiring as a well-respected member of the organization. While learning what he needed to learn was not fun, it was life changing.

Here's a question we can contemplate: can we learn "the hard stuff" without having to suffer hardships or disasters?

Perhaps the answer can be yes, *if*— and this is a big *if*— if you are willing to seek out the deeper truth and wisdom within you. Deeply rooted in your consciousness or soul or spirit is a source of wisdom you can access.

If the pilot in the above example, before being fired, had reached a point of self-exploration, he would have learned enough to give up his addiction, find his source of inner strength, and build his life gradually over time and keep his job. He could have learned these lessons without the fall from grace that he experienced.

I don't mean to imply that if you learn your deeper lessons you will avoid some of life's more difficult moments. But, rather, if such events happen, you will have the inner strength to navigate the episode and come out all right on the other side.

The Learning Process

Is the deeper aspect of your soul, or spirit, or higher self, or greater awareness trying to teach you something? If it were, how open would you be?

Most of us want to minimize conflict. We don't want to stir the waters. But, there is also a wonderful instinct in us to see what's at the bottom of the well, even when the waters are still. We have both tendencies, and, therefore, we must decide which one is more valuable to us.

If we choose to learn the deeper lessons life wants to teach us, how do it? Here are some suggestions:

• Be open

Imagine you have a CB radio, but you have the talk button locked on *send*. You are broadcasting, not receiving. One way of being open is to be in the receiving position. You may ask yourself questions like, "What do I need to learn?" "How can I develop?" "What are my next steps?" "What do I need to change about myself?" Then listen for the answer.

These types of questions are both questions and announcements. The content of the questions is clear and direct. The announcement you are making is, "Please understand, I am willing to learn whatever I need to learn."

• Set up a tension

Asking the types of questions listed above, and not trying to answer them with your own opinions, sets up a tension. Think of it as if you had a search engine in your mind. Once you ask these types of questions, your mind begins to access all the databanks to find the answers. You are doing your job by establishing the tension, and the mind is doing its job by getting your answer.

The most powerful motivation for learning is when it is generated by structural tension. The purpose for learning is to accomplish a goal, so the learning process is a strategic part of the action plan. The tension sets up a dynamic in which the learning takes on a special function. It serves to resolve the tension in favor of the fulfillment of the goal. It is a secondary choice to the primary choice of achieving the desired outcome we want to create. Further still, we can create structural tension when we define a learning goal. What do we want to learn, master, assimilate, acquire? Once we understand our learning goal, we can then acknowledge our current reality. Once structure tension is established, we are motivated to go through whatever steps, no matter how difficult, to reach our learning goal.

- Be in the un-know

You can't teach anyone anything if they think they already know the answer. Even if you think you've resolved these questions, go back to school, as it were. Become a student. Decide where you stand in terms of learning whatever life has to teach you. Instead of being in "the know," be in the "un-know". It will make your learning easier.

- Don't stop

Learning, especially in this form, is an ongoing, lifetime process. Don't stop learning once you have had your first few lessons. Dedicate yourself to being a student. Let the teachings come. Let them enrich and add to your life.

Learning Styles

Not everyone learns the same way. Some of us learn better by getting our hands into what we are doing, and some of us read the manual cover-to-cover before we begin to take action. Some of us prepare, and some of us experiment. Notice your own personal learning style.

When you are better acquainted with how you learn, you can work with your own rhythms and patterns. Here are some questions to help you assess your own learning styles:

- For those things you like learning, what is your typical pattern?

- For those things you don't like learning, what is your typical pattern?

- How well do you learn from others' examples?

- How well do you learn from personal involvement?

- How well do you learn when under a deadline?

- How well do you learn when there is no deadline?

- How well do you learn from your mistakes?

- How well do you learn from your successes?

- How well do you learn from other people's mistakes, successes?

Although all of us have some learning styles that we use most often, we may need at times to adopt a different learning style. You may be taking a class that teaches you how to use a new piece of computer software. The class instructor may have a very different approach to learning than you do. You may be able to use one of your learning styles in the situation, and if so, great. But you may have to use your instructor's learning approach to learn the software. If that's the case, it's best to switch gears and adapt to the instructor's learning style, rather than fight against it during the course.

Your life as art is a learning world, a world in which you learn by discovery, mistakes, successes, experiments, instruction, practice, exploration, study, analysis, and breakthroughs. You learn by your direct experience and vicariously through the experiences of others.

Learn to increase your learning potential, and you will be in a better position to create your life as art.

Creating a Health Strategy

Part of creating your life as art has to do with you as the creative force in your own life-building process. So let's take a moment to think about your health, because, to have the necessary stamina to create the life you want, you must manage your health.

It's Up To You

This is a funny age we live in. On the one hand, more and more of us are exercising, eating healthy diets, balancing our work lives with our personal lives, getting regular checkups, and getting enough rest and relaxation. But, at the same time, there is a higher number of us falling prey to diabetes, having problems with our weight, engaging in unhealthy life-style habits, eating poorly, being too sedentary, feeling pressure and stress in our lives, and feeling powerless and out of control. I suppose any period of time can claim that "it was the best of times; it was the worst of times." We're no exception.

The other day I was chatting with a friend who is about the same age as I am. We agreed that when we were kids, it seemed rare to find a very fat person. There were a few fat adults, but hardly any fat children. Now, there are many fat people of all ages. Is our memory wrong, or have the times changed?

There is nothing wrong with being fat in and of itself. Santa Claus is fat, and people around the world love him. But there is a health dimension to it. Your chances of illness are greater if you are overweight. Santa Claus doesn't have to worry about this problem because he is immortal. For the rest of us, we had better pay attention to what we are eating.

Health has a physical dimension. Some of us can't be healthy regardless of what we do. We can only make the best of it. I think of people like Stephen Hawking, the Nobel Prize winning physicist as well as author of *A Brief History of Time, A Universe in a Nutshell*, and many technical books on physics. Hawking is totally paralyzed by Amyotrophic Lateral Sclerosis, known as Lou Gehirg's disease. And yet, he has built his life around his work, partly through advances in technology, and entirely on his strength of character.

Another such person is Christopher Reeve who tragically fell from a horse, leaving him paralyzed. At first, after the accident, he thought about suicide. But, he made a choice to live. Even then he could have retired and spent the rest of his life feeling sorry for himself.

Instead, he has resumed being a true creator. He has become a force in supporting neuroscientists around the world in conquering the most complex diseases of the brain and central nervous system. He now directs films, writes books, acts, is chairman of the board of his own non-profit foundation, is Vice Chairman of the National Organization on Disability, helped Senator Jim Jeffords pass the Work Incentives Improvement Act, and on and on it goes. Instead of giving up, he added a new career of activist to his ongoing career as artist.

So many others are restricted by a limiting physical condition over which they have no control. And yet, they have found a way to create their lives in spite of their deficiencies.

If we are lucky enough to be able to improve our physical condition, we should take it if we want to be better creators of our lives. Many artists, musicians, actors, and all dancers train like athletes. In doing so, they are supporting their total creative act.

Diet

Physical health includes how you manage your diet. Most of us who grew up before the age of fast food and junk food didn't have to think about diet as children. When I was a kid I was as skinny as a bean poll, and yet I could eat anything, and as much as I wanted. When I reached my Thirties, I was shocked to discover that my metabolism had slowed down, and now I must make adjustments to my diet. Many of us have had to confront this real-ization.

While this is not a book on diet, you will be well served to review your eating habits. There are many good books on the shelves to read. Of course, they don't all agree, so pick ones that attract you. Experiment. Rosalind and I have tried many diets, from Barry Sears *The Zone*, to low-fat diet regiments of Dr. Dean Ornish, to the *Sugar Busters* approach of Steward, Bethea, Andrews and Balart. We weren't especially attracted to the Atkin's diet, but we know people who like it very much.

About three years ago we tried out the Suzanne Somers diet, and then found the work of Michel Montignac whose work seems to have influenced Somers' approach. The Somers and Montignac diets have worked best for us. We have lost over twenty-five pounds each, and have been able to maintain a constant weight for over three years as of this writing.

Of course, there is an abundance of opinion about diet, and often, common wisdom changes. How can you decide what to do? Do what makes sense. Good sound medical advice is always a good rule-of-thumb. Talk to your doctor. Just remember, not all doctors agree. Some of them haven't updated themselves about the new data available in the field of nutrition.

Find something that is *both* a good healthy practice and that is doable. So many good things are so disruptive to our lives that there is little chance we can maintain the practice. The easier it is to do, the more likely it is that we can do it.

Rosalind and I like the diet we now follow because it works for us, our general overall health has improved using it, and we can do it easily at home or on the road. Doing it on the road has been very important to us because we travel a lot. Also, while Michel Montignac has a very insightful explanation of why his ideas work well, Susanne Somers' recipes are just sensational.

To Sleep, Perchance To Dream

Sleep is restorative. There are the physical benefits. And there is also a structural benefit that comes from dreaming.

Throughout the day, your mind is taking in many forms of information. Some you understand on a conscious level, some on a subliminal level.

There is a mix of inputs that come through all of your senses. You see, hear, touch, smell, and taste. You have a mix of sensations. You have thoughts, feelings, intuitions, and various concepts that you use as a matrix with which to sense the world. You also have memory of the past and imagination about the future.

Tens of thousands of these factors merge in a complex of threads. Your mind retains this complex and begins to labor over it. These threads don't knit together into a comprehensive whole. Instead, they are like a badly designed puzzle in which the parts never fit together. And yet, your mind wants to resolve the differences.

The mind wants things to add up; it wants to bring order out of chaos. So when you sleep, your mind begins to address some of the chaos by resolving the discrepancies through dreams.

The dream is like a film in which some of the parts that can't fit are made to interact. The nice thing about the mind is that its film doesn't have to be true to life. Strange relationships, absurd events, impossible physics, and improbable episodes can flow quite easily from moment to moment. The plot doesn't have to make sense from a cinematic point of view or any other point of view. All it has to do is relieve some of the chaos for a while.

Dreaming takes many forms. Sometimes your dreams are prophetic and are able to prepare you for the future. Some dreams can predict events before they actually happen. Some dreams express forms of anxiety. Some dreams are sexual.

Almost all dreams, no matter what their nature, are ways the mind tries to resolve tension. The tension sometimes has an emotional dimension. But, more importantly, it has a structural dimension. Remember, a structure is a whole entity in which the parts of the structure impact each other. If they don't fit, they rub against each other in a type of battle. The mind wants to bring peace to the warring factions and restore order.

This tendency of the mind to attempt to resolve tension is why you can be so inventive and creative once you have established structural tension. You have enlisted your mind in the cause, and it will generate ingenious ideas that will help resolve the structural tension.

But there is more going on in your life than just your focus on *what you want,* and *what you have.* You are bombarded with stimulus. MTV has nothing on your mind in terms of the amount of multiple data, quick cuts, simultaneous sensation, and concurrent perception that it is processing constantly. But, after a while, your mind needs a little relief from the commotion. Dreams help create a temporary respite from the daily drum solo of input.

After you have had a nightmare in which the worst possible things have happened to you, you can awake in the morning actually refreshed. The nightmare has taken your worst fears and played them out. Even though the script was the least desired resolution of your fears, there is a type of resolution. The resolution is not about the content of the dream. The nightmare always has terrible content and is almost always left unresolved. What is resolved is the structure. The parts have been made to fit. They have been let out to play, as it were, and by developing their own direction and rhythm, clashing against each other, and letting things get out of hand, movement has transpired. Some of the competing tensions have been resolved through the mind's filmmaking. And that's why a nightmare often can bring release and renewal.

Of course, we hate nightmares. But, fortunately, our mind doesn't care and will continue to generate them when the chaotic noise gets too high.

Other dreams, the ones that are nicer to have, also give us resolution of tensions the mind has collected. But what happens when we do not dream?

We begin to feel a type of stress. We become exhausted, drained, depleted, and jaded. Sleep that doesn't include dreaming won't help. We need to dream so the mind has a chance to sort itself out.

If you have sleep problems, find ways to overcome them. These days, much is known that can help you. Sleep clinics, books, internet sites focusing on sleep, and medical treatments are available. Sleeping pills aren't always a good answer because they often prevent dreaming. So find ways to dream, which is one of the functions of a healthy and restorative sleep.

Mental Health

To create mental health, cultivate true interests, have an intellectual challenge, develop mental discipline, have a good balance of times when you're active and when you're passive, have a sense of seriousness, and have a sense of humor.

This is not all there is, of course, but it's a very good foundation. Mental health, like other forms of health, is advanced by the actions you take. Use your mind. Rethink everything. Read books with which you don't agree. Read books that don't agree with each other. Recently, I read a book by the Dalai Lama at the same time as a book by Jean Paul Sartre. A Buddhist and an existentialist is an interesting match. As I read these two diverse viewpoints I wasn't trying to see who was right and who was wrong. I was enjoying these two brilliant points of view, juxtaposed to each other. Of course Sartre was an atheist, and the Dalai Lama isn't. Both were very convincing. And I loved their minds, the way they put their ideas together, and the richness of their respective approaches. For me it was as if I were spending time with these two remarkable people. I wasn't interested in incorporating the way they see the world into my viewpoint. I just wanted to hang out, which is something we can do, thanks to the written word.

If you are depressed, you will have few interests. If you begin to develop interests, you may still be depressed, but at least you have a better way to spend some of your time than simply suffering. I am not talking about clinical depression, which is a condition that needs to be addressed through professional help. I am talking about the normal type of depression that all of us go through from time to time. The type of depression that gave birth to the blues. "My man done left me, and I'm feeling mighty low" kind of depression.

Finding interests has a push-pull effect. At first you are pushing yourself, jump starting your interests, but then, you begin to be pulled along by the attractiveness of the interest.

Sometimes, the best interests to develop are atypical from what you normally do. If you are a physical type, do something artistic or intellectual. If you are an intellectual or artistic type, do something physical.

I'm the artistic intellectual type. I create photographs, compose music for hours on end in my fantastic electronic music studio, make films, write books, read poetry, go to art exhibits, etc. I also love to read books and my favorite magazine *The New Yorker*. So, in the winter I ski, and in the summer I swim. Swimming and skiing take me out of my head. The trip away is great for my head because whenever I return to my artistic life, I am renewed.

Change is the nature of rejuvenation. If you work at a desk job, take an adventurous vacation. Go on safari, swim with the dolphins, climb a mountain, go on a bike trip through the English countryside. If you live an active life, hang out on the beach in Hawaii, go to a health spa, go to a meditation retreat, or watch TV non-stop for a week or two. It doesn't really matter what you do. What matters is that you are recharging the batteries by putting yourself in an atypical situation.

We need that from time to time. So, if you don't build it in, chances are it won't happen.

Humor is a must. Humor is based on a few different important things. One is a change of perspective. Humor takes all of our constructs, pretenses, and fixed points of view, and turns them around. Another type of humor shows us irony at its best. We can laugh at ourselves, and that takes the pressure off our misconception of having to be perfect.

The type of humor that is best for mental health is one in which we can laugh at ourselves as an example of the human condition. The type of humor that is less useful from a mental health point of view is humor at the expense of others; this type of joke often tries to ridicule another's weakness and to put us above other people.

Jokes are little tension-resolution systems. The set up for the joke leads us toward a certain expectation. That's the tension. But, the punch line is not what we expected. That's the resolution. But studies have shown that most people can anticipate the punch line, and yet they laugh anyway. This is because the joke has such a good structure. We laugh at jokes we have already heard. Why? Certainly not because we are surprised by the punch line. We laugh because we are enjoying the structure of the joke and love living for the moment in the crazy world that the joke inhabits. Listening to a great joke, even one we have known for years, is a little like listening to Mozart. The structure is so wonderful we could hear it again and again.

What's very healthy is to crack jokes. Some people think that cracking jokes is a defense mechanism to protect oneself against the hostile and threatening world. Sometimes it is. But more often than not, it is a way of naming the incongruities of life. One of the best parts of my relationship with Rosalind is that we both crack jokes. Often, we are the only ones who get each other's jokes. Thank God we have each other.

After we crack a bunch of jokes, the world seems like a better place, we enjoy each other's company even more, and we have shared a type of intimacy that's hard to explain. We feel closer to each other and to the world itself. Everyone has at least one joke they know how to tell. My grandmother had one. She would tell it about three or four times a year at family gatherings. I can still see the joy in her face when she told her joke. This was my grandmother's joke that brought such moments of joy to her:

> There were two brothers who went fishing every Saturday. They would fish all day, but one brother caught all the fish. The other never got even a bite. After years of this, one Saturday the brother who caught all the fish was sick and couldn't go fishing. The other brother saw his chance. He rowed out to their usual fishing spot, put down the anchor, set up his lines, and began to fish. He fished from morning to night. Not one bite. Dejected, he pulled up anchor and began to row toward shore. As he was leaving, a little fish put its head out of the water and called, "Hey, where's your brother!"

My grandmother would laugh and laugh, and so would we. We knew the joke, but it was still fun to hear her tell it again and share her joy at the telling of it.

Creating a Health Strategy

Many people in the health field are now using structural tension in their work. One of the most notable is Dr. Peter Boggs, a renowned international expert on asthma. Dr. Boggs uses structural tension charts with his patients, defining health goals, current reality, and the action plans that enable them to accomplish their health goals. He has achieved outstanding success, and his work is becoming a major influence within the field of asthma.

Dr. Judith Boice, a naturopathic physician and acupuncturist, is the author of *"But My Doctor Never Told Me That!": Secrets for*

Creating Lifelong Health. She encourages patients to examine why they want to be healthy and to define their own personal vision of health. In her practice she introduces patients to structural tension as a way of helping them achieve their health vision. She wisely has linked creating health with the creative process. Here's how Dr. Boice has described her process:

> One of the first questions I ask a new patient is "Are you interested in being healthy?" Many look at me quizzically. "Well, of course I do. Why else would I be here?"
>
> For most people, health is a necessary prerequisite to create what truly matters to them. Without health, they cannot bring their visions to fruition. Not everyone is interested in being healthy, however. Some simply want symptomatic relief. Others are running from diseases they fear. A few pursue health to appease a mate or parent.
>
> Your motivation for choosing health impacts your ability to create health. Choosing health to serve your life vision fundamentally differs from avoiding illness, problem solving, or pleasing others.
>
> If someone wants to be healthy, my next question is "And what would full health look like for you?" I can't offer anyone a meaningful one-size-fits-all definition of health. For one of my patients, "health" means completing two iron man competitions a year. Another wants a positive outlook on life — she's been clinically depressed for years — and enough energy to work in the garden when she gets home from work. Each of these visions has power for that individual, but not necessarily for anyone else.
>
> I encourage patients to include enough detail so they can accurately measure when they have achieved their desired state of health. "I want to lower my blood pressure," for example, is a very fuzzy end result. "I want to have blood pressure

readings of 125/80 five days a week" is a very clear-ly defined goal.

Our next step is to define their current state of health, focusing on the details that pertain to their picture of health. Most doctors' visits begin here, with current symptoms, *not* someone's vision of health. This method aims at eliminating symptoms, not creating health.

For those who truly desire health, I encourage them to formally choose their vision of health. Many people follow all kinds of health-promoting regimens without actually choosing to be healthy. Often they are not even sure what health means to them. Without a clear vision of health, how could they decide if they are doing enough or too much, or evaluate if their current routine is improving or undermining their health?

The process of clarifying and then choosing your vision of health helps focus your efforts. You can also more accurately evaluate the results, e.g. did your diet and exercise routine help you lose fat without sacrificing muscle? Did the dietary changes lower your total cholesterol below 200? Have the biofeedback sessions reduced or eliminated your headaches? Of course the questions you ask will depend on your particular definition of health.

You can establish structural tension for your health goals, quality of health, and overall health condition, and then, take the actions that will support the accomplishment of your health vision. With structural tension as your foundation, you will find it easier to take the needed actions over sustained periods.

The Foundations of Health

Many people wanting to improve their health focus on vita-mins, minerals, herbs, and homeopathic remedies. While these supplements can play a vital role in restoring and maintaining health, they cannot take the place of good lifestyle choices. The daily decisions you make build the foundation for health: what you eat, whether you exercise and take time to relax, and what kind of environment you live and work in. Here is Dr. Boice's list of useful factors in creating health:

NUTRITION

• Choose foods as close as possible to their natural state. Have you ever seen a Twinkie® bush or a Coca-Cola® river?

• Select local, seasonal produce. Foods ripen in a cyclical pattern that supports seasonal needs in your body. The liver, for example, works hard throughout the winter when we tend to eat heavier, oilier foods to stay warm. The bitter greens that announce spring (e.g. dandelion and arugula) cleanse and support liver function.

• Choose organic produce whenever possible. Studies show organic products contain about 70% more nutrients than their conventionally grown counterparts. Organic farming methods also improve the health of the soil and minimize environmental hazards (see the section on environmental health below).

• Separate fruits from other foods by at least one hour. Fruits move quickly through the digestive tract, usually within one to two hours. Eating other foods at the same time slows the progress of the fruit, which begins to putrefy in the digestive tract causing gas, bloating, and sometimes cramping. Melons digest most quickly and should be eaten alone. The classic summer picnic of hamburgers, coleslaw and potato salad topped off with watermelon is a recipe for digestive disaster.

• Eat foods that support *your* body. Work with someone who can help tailor your diet for your particular needs. An extremely high protein diet, for example, may benefit one person and wreak havoc for another.

EXERCISE

• A complete program includes aerobic, strength building, stretching, and agility exercise.

• When beginning an exercise program, always do LESS than you think you can. Many people begin too quickly, strain or tear muscles, and are too sore to move for weeks. "I'll never exercise again!" vows the limping weekend warrior. Do yourself a favor: build up slowly. If you haven't exercised for several years, begin by walking 5 minutes a day. Yes, 5 minutes a day. Add 2 - 3 minutes each week. This conservative approach will reward you in the long run.

• Aerobic exercise conditions the cardiovascular system and improves endurance. The minimum amount of aerobic exercise to *maintain* aerobic conditioning is 20 minutes, 3 times a week.

• Strength-building exercise, e.g. calisthenics and light weight lifting, increases muscle mass. If you are sedentary, after age 35 – 40 you will lose 1 pound of muscle a year and gain 1.5 pounds of fat. At rest a pound of muscle burns 32 calories a day. A pound of fat burns 2 calories per day. Each year you lose muscle and replace it with fat, your metabolic rate (how quickly you burn calories) slows. You can reverse this trend by including strength-building exercise in your routine, e.g. 10 minutes 3 or 4 times a week. The older you are, the more important strength building exercise becomes.

• Stretching limbers muscles and lubricates joints. Stretching also cues strained or damaged muscle tissue to repair normally. Without stretching, muscles repair by laying down a tangled mass of scar tissue, which over time reduces flexibility and range of motion.

• Agility exercises, such as standing on one leg or walking across a log, fine tunes balance and coordination.

• Focus on the things you love. When asked what activities she enjoyed, one patient confided she loved to dance. I encouraged her to dance as part of her exercise routine. "You mean dancing counts as exercise?" she asked, surprised. Physical activities that you love still count as exercise.

RELAXATION

• Two nervous systems, the sympathetic and parasympathetic, run simultaneously in your body. The sympathetic predominates when you are stressed, preparing the body to fight or run away. The parasympathetic nervous system prevails when you are relaxed and at peace. Healing and regeneration occur only when the parasympathetic nervous system is dominant.

• Take short relaxation breaks during the day. Three to five minutes of deep breathing or a "relaxation shower" (releasing all of the muscles from head to toe) can shift the balance toward the parasympathetic nervous system and allow healing and rejuvenation to occur.

ENVIRONMENTAL HEALTH

• Healthy people require a healthy environment for living and working. You cannot breathe toxic fumes, drink polluted water, work all day under florescent lights, and still expect to maintain good health.

• Avoid xenoestrogens. "Xeno" means "foreign," so xenoestrogens are foreign substances that act like estrogen in the body. Estrogen's basic message to cells is "divide, divide, divide." In normal amounts, estrogen stimulates growth. In excess, estrogen triggers tumor formation. The epidemic of breast, uterine, ovarian, testicular, and prostate cancer is a sad reflection of xenoestrogen pollution. What are these substances that mimic estrogen in the body? Chiefly chlorine and chloride-containing chemicals, e.g. insecticides, pesticides, and off gassing from plastics. The most potent carcinogen known is dioxin, a chlorine-based chemical used to bleach paper white.

• Invest in a good water filter, one that eliminates chlorine, solvents, and heavy metals.

• Spend at least 20 minutes a day in the sunshine. The pineal gland requires full-spectrum light exposure (without glasses or contacts) to stimulate normal seratonin production. Seratonin stabilizes moods, regulates carbohydrate metabolism, and stabilizes sleep cycles. Seasonal Affective Disorder (depression that begins in the autumn and improves in spring) is associated with reduced light exposure and diminished seratonin production. Short sun exposure benefits the body; too much promotes skin cancer. Use sunscreen lotion on the face, neck, hands, and other exposed areas. Products are now rated using a standard called "Solar

Protection. Factor," or SPF. To figure how long your sun-screen will protect you, multiply the sun exposure time without burning (usually 10 - 15 minutes for a fair skinned person who is not used to being in the sun) by the SPF and divide by 2. If you are using a lotion with SPF 8, for example, the formula would be 10 (minutes) X 8 (SPF) ÷ 2 = 40 minutes of safe sun protection. Keep in mind that you can NOT reapply the sunscreen at the end of 40 minutes and prolong your sun protection. Remember that your lips also need sun protection. Look for lip balms with SPF ratings on the package.

• If you have chronic respiratory problems, e.g. hay fever, sinusitis, or asthma, consider investing in a good air filter. You won't eliminate the cause of your reactivity, but you can reduce the amount of pollen, dust, and other irritants in the air.

• Choose to live at least half a mile from high-tension electrical wires, television or radio stations, or microwave towers, all of which can disrupt your body's own electromagnetic field. Electric blankets also generate a detrimental electromagnetic field and are associated with increased rates of leukemia, especially in children.

•Ultimately your body is the part of the earth you are most directly responsible for. Your body is your Earth. This extraordinary vehicle is in many ways a microcosm of the planet. The healthier the planet, the healthier your body can be. Much of the information in this section suggests how to protect yourself from environmental damage, e.g. filter the water and avoid chemicals. The deepest "cure" is to support the health of our environment, for its sake as well as our own.

Whose Job Is It?

Too often, we think about our bodies as if they were the same as automobiles. If they have something wrong, take them to the garage and ask the mechanic to fix them. We put the responsibility on the doctors rather than ourselves. We think somehow that we can neglect our bodies until they need repair. We then take them into our garage (medical center) and say, "Okay, it's your job to make us better." This is a fool hardy attitude.

Jerry Brown, the maverick politician and former governor of California, once made the most interesting comment on public health issues I have ever heard. When asked his opinion of pub- licly- funded health care, he said, "You smoke, you eat the wrong foods, you don't exercise, you live an unhealthy life style, and you want me to pay for it?" Not to enter into a discussion about pub- lic policy in the context of this book, and while I generally think it makes some sense for a society to help out those who can't afford the overwhelming expense of adequate health care, I think that Jerry Brown made an interesting point. Who is in charge of our health. What is our role in creating health? What are the conse- quences of not taking a more active part in the creation of our health condition? What is our role in the process? If the time comes when we need health care treatment, we may be reaping the consequences we sowed through our lifestyle choices.

Creating health is better than healing illness. This is not to say that there is anything wrong with taking advantage of medical sci- ence's advances. It is only to ask the rhetorical question, isn't it bet- ter to live in ways that lead to a better and healthier path?

Chapter 16

People

While creating our life as art requires an independence from our prevailing circumstances, if we can create a supportive atmosphere for ourselves, we make our job easier. This supportive atmosphere includes having the right tools for the job we've taken on, working conditions that are free of distractions, and a pleasant ambience.

One of the most substantial characteristics of our ambience and working conditions are the people in our lives. The fact is that everyone is everyone else's environment.

Who are these people? Do they support us, or are they neutral? Perhaps they are opposed to what we are trying to accomplish, or antagonistic to us as individuals.

We can work in neutral and even hostile environments and still create those things that matter to us. History is filled with champions who have not let the animosity of others stop their creative process.

Beethoven, having written one of his greatest masterpieces— *The Grosso Fugue* for string quartet—said, after the performers he originally wrote it for had rejected it as unplayable, "I write this music for a future time." It is now one of the most played of his compositions for string quartet.

Buckminster Fuller, one of the greatest geniuses of his generation, worked in isolation for most of his life. In the latter part of his life, his very original and visionary work began to attract an audience. But, up to that point, he had to learn to be self-generating and self-reliant which made it possible for him to do his most innovative and influential work while living in an age that did not understand or appreciate his work.

Decca Records rejected the Beatles.

Robert Frost couldn't get published in the United States until his forties. He had to travel to England to publish his first book.

Galileo was forced to renounce his own work by the church.

Management giant W. Edwards Deming was another prophet who had to leave his country for his work to become popular. His methodology was ignored in the West until the Japanese made significant inroads in world markets using his approach to building quality into the manufacturing process.

Many accomplished men and women were rejected before they were recognized and acclaimed.

It may turn out that very few people understand what you are trying to create. And if that's the case, you need to learn how to build your own sympathetic infrastructure that gives you support and nourishment.

A Rule of Thumb

Here's the rule of thumb many creators have learned: *Surround yourself with people who support you, support what you are doing, and root for your success. Avoid people who do not support you, do not understand you, do not like you, do not wish you well, and would like nothing better than to watch you fall on your ass.*

Your world is made up of people who are on your side, those who are neutral, and those who are not on your side. Who do you want to invite to your party?

Some people are more like filmmakers, and some are more like film critics. The film critics often tell the filmmakers how they didn't do it right. The filmmakers never invite the film critic on the set. Films are made by filmmakers not film critics. This principle was expressed by many people in the human potential movement this way: games are played by players; get the spectators off the field.

The image of trying to play a game with people who are not playing, just watching, is striking. The spectators get in the way, don't help, and take up needed space on the field. It's a good idea to know who is a player and who is a spectator.

If we allow those who are not interested in our success to fill our psychic, emotional, mental, and spiritual space, we pollute our own environment.

This is not to say that people who criticize our creations are not supportive. Sometimes the best support you can get from your friends is an astute critique. But, we need to choose credible people to play that role, people who truly wish us success, and not people who do not.

This was a point that Stephen King made in his wonderful book *On Writing*. When he works on a book project, there are only a few people he will let read his work—his wife and a few friends he trusts. He has learned not to show his work to those who do not understand or support him. He wants a third-party opinion, but the type that will help him reach his goal, the type that will add to his creative process.

It's important to carefully pick who you let into your creative process. They must be truthful. But that's not enough. They also must have valuable insight that enables you to adjust, improve, grow, and become more effective. And they must be on your side.

There's nothing like surrounding yourself with people who actually like you just the way you are— people who are not trying to improve you, change you, manipulate you, save you, etc.

There is a line. On one side of the line are those who will give you the news—good, bad, and indifferent. They care about you and your success.

On the other side of the line are those who do not actually care about you and have motives other than true support. Perhaps your success makes them feel they should have done more with their lives. Perhaps the way you go about creating your goals argues against their worldviews, their concept of how the world works, or their life experiences.

While the line can seem thin and hard to detect, it is actually wide and obvious when we look closely. It's not always easy to identify the line because the behavior can almost be identical for each group. The key word here is *almost*. When you are with people who are on the unsupportive side of the line, the after-effect will feel hollow. You will not feel momentum, energy, growth, drive, or vitality. You will feel somewhat depleted. When, however, you're with people on the supportive side of the line, you will experience dynamic propulsion, even when they have picked apart what you have done. Their words have the impact of support, because the words are given in the context of furthering your cause.

Making a Tough Choice

From time to time you will need to rethink who you allow into your life. You are not obligated to surround yourself with those who would just as soon see you fail.

The mathematics of every relationship is this: it takes two to say *yes*, it only takes one to say *no*. Perhaps there are those to whom you need to say *no*. To no longer have these people in your life may be an important secondary choice to your primary choice of the life you want to build.

I know this is hard advice. You may feel a conflict of emotions when it comes to the people in your life. You may love them, like them, wish them success, want to be supportive, want to be a good friend. But, if they do not support you on some very basic level, you may need to see them less often.

You take this action, not because you don't like them, but because you support your own life building process more.

Sometimes you need to take a stand in favor of yourself. Sometimes you need to change the cast of players with whom you surround yourself. This may be one of the most strategic choices you can make on behalf of your own well-being.

In and Out

Many people come in and out of our lives. They join us at just the right time and then move on. They may be there for only a short moment, and yet they become important to us. They remain a significant twinkling of memory, even though we will never see them again.

I remember many of the people we met while camping across America and Canada. People we would meet around a camp fire in the middle of the wilderness. Like the couple we met who had retired, had redesigned a moving truck as a homemade RV before there were many RVs, and registered it in Florida because that was the cheapest place to reside at the time. They had a TV and a bathtub in that thing (not a shower but a real bathtub). We had a little mountain tent, and to us, they were living in the lap of the most exquisite luxury. We knew them for one afternoon and one evening. They talked about their former lives as middle-class professionals from Wisconsin who had decided to roam the country when they no longer had to earn a living. They were modern-day nomads, free as the wind, happy with each other, glad to share an evening of good talk around a campfire in the middle of a cool fall Wyoming night, filled with the wisdom of life that even we, then in our twenties, could so clearly understand. That night there was no generation gap, just two pairs of contented vagabonds, old and young, touching each other's life for a brief moment of the sweetness of human contact. And then moving on.

Wondrous Relationships

There's another way that people come in and out of our lives, and that's when we establish structural tension. When we are aware and committed to the outcome we want to create, are fluent in the current reality as it changes, and as we hold the tension between the desired state and the actual state, something wondrous can begin to happen. People who can play an important part in our creative process begin to appear in our lives.

In chapter 2 we talked about the extra-normal experiences that can happen when we are creating. Strange coincidences, magical and happy accidents, extraordinary events suddenly seem to help the cause. One of the most common of these miraculous developments is how people come into your life to join you in the creative process. Everyone who creates has many stories of the right person somehow "showing up" at just the right time, bringing with him or her just the piece that was needed to move the creation along. Many professional creators count on it after a while. They don't know who it will be, how they will enter the picture, what role they will play, or how long they will be on the scene, but they know these "right" people will come at just the right time. And sure enough, they do.

Joseph Jaworski, in his book *Synchronicity*, says, "The people who come to you are the very people you need in relation to your commitment. Doors open, a sense of flow develops, and you find you are acting in a coherent field of people who may not even be aware of one another. You are not acting individually any longer, but out of the unfolding generative order. This is the unbroken wholeness of the implicate order out of which seemingly discrete events take place. At this point, your life becomes a series of predictable miracles."

Let miracles happen to you. Allow for the possibility that there is more in play in the creative process and in life than meets the eye. But, realize that these miracles do not come from simply being passive and hoping something will happen. Miracles happen not by "letting go" but rather by broadening the creative process to include what you can control and what you can influence but cannot directly control. The phenomenon of synchronicity is not independent from your action, but it is an indirect outcome of your action. Had you not done your work, the miracle could not have been evoked. If you set your creative process in motion, dimensions beyond your control, but not beyond your influence, will begin to emerge with startling regularity. Our life will be filled with people with whom we unite for the moment of creation. They may continue to be life-long friends. Or they may drift out of our lives and on to their next mission.

People come and go through our lives. We come and go through their lives. Often, we may feel that we must stay in contact. We try. But, as time moves, we hopelessly and inevitably drift from each other. We can't help it. The moment we were meant to be together is over. If we try to hold on past its own special moment, we find ourselves becoming artificial.

It's okay to let it go. This is not our usual understanding. We think if we were so close, it must last. We can think that the closeness was an illusion if it *doesn't last*. Our thoughts deceive us. The time we had together was real and true and great. That it had its own time, and that that time has past, doesn't deny the depth of relationship that we savored in the moment.

Like most, my life is filled with very special people. Some have been there for the moment, and some have been friends year after year.

Some, even though we may not see each other for months, years, and perhaps decades, are always close. The moment of reunion is never strange or forced. It's as if we had seen each other the day before. While we have developed our own lives, some everlasting and unchanging bond of continuity seems to persist.

These types of relationships are ongoing and growing, even though our actual contact may be periodic.

We are on loan to each other. The real miracle is that we can come together for a time and be so inextricably involved in each other's lives.

The Freedom to Choose

The phenomenon we have been talking about involves the gift of free choice we have been given. We choose to dedicate ourselves to our own creations. That choice galvanizes a process in which people may appear in our lives. Yet once they are there, we make a choice to be involved, to let them into our process, to join in and play a role. We could say no to them. That would be one choice. We can say yes to them, and that's another choice. Still, we must choose one way or the other.

I love the old story of the man who believes in God with undying faith. When a flood comes and the water begins to rise and rise, he is forced to climb on the roof of his house. Civil defense sends a boat to rescue him. He refuses to go and tells his would be saviors that he has faith in God and that everything will be all right. He then refuses the helicopter that attempts to rescue him. The water keeps rising until the roof is now underwater, and he is not able to keep his head above it. In a last ditch effort, the Coast Guard sends a small submarine to save the drowning man. The man waves off the sub and tries to say, "Don't worry, I believe in God." As his last words are uttered, more bubbles than sound, he drowns. He wakes up at the gates of Saint Peter. When he realizes where he is, he really gets mad. "I had faith in God, and what does he do? Drowns me!" Saint Peter shakes his head, smiles, and says to the man, "God sent you a boat, a helicopter and a sub. What more do you want!"

We can choose to allow ourselves to be supported by those who come to help us or not. And I'm reminded of the classic line in Howard Hawks production of *To Have Or Have Not* when Lauren Bacall kisses Bogart for the first time. "Why did you do that," Bogart asks. "I wanted to see if I liked it," purrs Bacall. "What do you think?" Bogart asks. "I don't know yet." Bacall answers. She kisses him again, moves away, and says, "It's even better when you help."In life, it's even better when we let others help. But remember, not everyone wants to help.

By choosing to have only those who support us in our creating environment, we open the space for miracles to happen. If we are filling our lives with those who are not on our side, there is little room for those who want to support us. That is one reason why it is so important to choose whom you want to let in. Let in those who want to create with you. Choose the creators over the critics. Choose those who add to the process. Avoid those who want to take away from the process. Choose those who give you energy, avoid those who are energy-draining. These types of choices set the stage for new people to come into your life at just the right time.

When we choose to join together, we create an authentic community. As Thomas Jefferson taught us, community is a collection of strong, free, and independent individuals who join together to build something more than any one of us could build alone. But at the core of it all is free choice. We are not forced to be together. We choose to, out of our desire to join with others for our common good. This principle is just as true in our own lives in the communities we build around us. Your life as art can be filled with people who have chosen to join together in support of each other's aspirations. We can play a central role in each other's creative process.

Here are two important points: Surround yourself with people who truly support you and your cause, and not with those who don't; and, let people come into your life who may play a pivotal role as part of your expansive creative process.

The relationship between these two principles is this: when you make the choice to join with those who support you, you open up the world to people who want to, and they will come in the perfect moment.

Chapter 17

Creating Your Life as Art

M y friend David Benelo is a walking work of art. He is a hair stylist who runs one of the most interesting salons in Montreal. David set up his salon with a European style café, full of little tables and chairs. The café serves the most delicious croissants, espressos or cappuccinos. Posters of films like Fellini's *La Dolce Vita,* or stills of Claudia Cardinale, Marcelo Mastroianni, and Sophia Loren evoke a sense of theater and charm. The music you hear may be classical, jazz, rock, or new wave, but it will always be hip. This isn't for effect, but because David knows and loves music.

The moment you arrive, you enter David's universe, international in spirit and, in fact, a cultural melting pot, people from all over the world landing at the same place at the same time and joining together in what everyone knows will be a jubilant rendezvous. The U.N. could learn a lesson or two from spending an hour at David's salon.

When you have your hair done by David you receive so much more than just a styling.... there are special moments of insights, fun, warmth and light.

As Moroccan Jews, David and his family experienced increased prejudice and discrimination throughout the Nineteen-Sixties. He immigrated to Canada and created a sensation in the world of style, his salon becoming one of the trendiest in Montreal. Eventually he managed to bring his whole family to Canada, well out of harms way.

David was a guest on one of our TV shows. We brought our cameras to David's salon, and Rosalind interviewed him while he cut her hair. While we were shooting, the phone rang. David picked it up and carried on a conversation in French while he con-tinued to cut Rosalind's hair with the confident hand of the mas-ter he is. After a number of "oui, oui, oui's," he hung up.

Here is some of the dialogue they then had while David cut Rosalind's hair:

Rosalind: When you are on the phone you always say yes to everyone...

David: It is so easy to say yes than to say no. When you say yes you provoke a reason to do something. When you say no, you cut everything off. There's no involvement, no continuation. When you say yes, you give a chance to have some-thing happen.

Rosalind: What is your concept of the creative process with hair and with life?

David: I don't follow the styles. I create the styles. There is a difference. I look at the person and I can tell her, "Your hair should be that way." She may have another vision when she first comes to see me. I am going to show her my vision by words so she can see the picture of what I want to give to her.

Rosalind: So you know exactly what you want to create if your client says yes.

David: If people allow me, I am 99.9% sure that the person will love what I am going to give her. My most beautiful reward is when I can give you something different...for your hair of course...but also, so you can realize something about life.

I had many times a client sitting and not saying a word. I keep following their way of being. I respect the way they are and once in a while I just throw away words and try to find out exactly what kind of spirit she has...and it's very funny...you can give a haircut to someone, and suddenly you realize they are not happy with themselves...and you try to provoke inside them what can make them happy.

It's not only cutting hair, cutting hair is one thing, but to make people happy or have them leave the shop happy is the most beautiful thing. I'm looking for something we can create through hair.

That's what is so fantastic about it. There is always something that connects us. Every individual is unique. Most of the time we realize that we have something to connect us. You have that spiritual feeling inside you and you have that smile that comes out that shows on your face.

We ended this segment with a close up on David's very beautiful face.

Once, while I was directing a film, one of the actors reported to the set with a hairstyle that was inappropriate for his role. It was a Sunday, and we were to begin our shoot on the Monday. I called David for help. David, his wife Silvana, Silvana's mother, and two other friends hopped into a car and traveled the five hours it took to get to our location in Vermont. Not only did he give the actor a perfect hairstyle for the movie we were making, but he also did his magic for the two women leads and another male lead. We invited his group to stay with us for as long as they wanted, but David and family hopped back into the car, his mission accomplished, and drove the five hours back to Montreal. And I had to beg him to take payment for his work, which he was going to "donate to the cause." I'm sure the trip down and back was a fun experience for David's party because David always makes whatever is going on an adventure.

David is typical of a person whose life *itself* is an art form. From very difficult circumstances, he created the life he now lives. He is doing work that is meaningful to him. He is surrounded by love, the love of his family and friends, but also the love of his clients and acquaintances. He is always into something. A new CD, a new film, a new meditation method, a book he has just read, a new restaurant to try, a new approach to hairstyling. He creates his own attractive environment, his own special world. His world has true sense of community, fun, involvement, energy, optimism, hope, connection, and above all, the creative process as a living, breathing, vital force in life.

We might think of David as a person who is blessed. In a way, he is. One definition of the word *blessing* is *bringing out the highest potential in a situation.*

Your life is blessed. You have the prospect of bringing out the highest potential in the circumstances of your life, even when the situation may be difficult at first. The blessing we are given is not provided to us fully matured and perfectly whole. Instead, we are supplied with the raw material. What do we want to create? How can we invent ways to achieve our vision, given the circumstances we find ourselves in? What chances are there for us to be involved with life. The time we have is a blessing.

The Counterpoint of Time

We move in a counterpoint of time.

As I write these words, I am present in the moment I am writing. As you read these words, the moment I wrote them is over. So, while I was there (the past for you, the present for me as I write this), I was also living in the your future, (this moment for you right now). Sorry if this is confusing. It's a little hard to express this idea, even though it seems very clear to me. Let me summarize the point: I knew these words would be read in the future, even as I experienced them in their moment of creation.

We create in the moment, but our creations often reach fruition on into the future. We are not trapped in just the moment. We are not just impulsively creative beings who cannot have a sense of future. While we create in the moment, the subject of our creative process is often events or conditions that will reach maturity over time, well beyond the moments we create them. Therefore, when we create, we live in at least two dimensions of time. We simultaneously are here (current reality) and there (our vision), in the future. Our current creative acts will lead to future creations. Now is the time that we connect with our future. And if we want our future to be a product of our creative process, now is the time we can begin to bring our vision into being. Now is the time we establish structural tension, the dynamic that will lead to the future we want to create.

Time is often our medium. Here's a story that illustrates the point. I was attending a strategic planning meeting for one of my corporate clients. The morning was filled with a fairly technical discussion about market trends, competition, organizational development as related to the business strategy, and departmental roles and accountabilities. Stuff, I must admit, I love. There's nothing like a group of senior execs, working at the top of their professional game, mapping out their plans for the future. The exercise can be one of the most exhilarating and creative there is. After some fairly intense work, we took a short coffee break.

The meeting took place on the second floor of a San Francisco hotel overlooking a sidewalk. As I looked out the window from our meeting room, I saw something fascinating. People walking on the sidewalk, the bright sunlight still low in the sky, caused long purple shadows to move across the pavement. It was a dance of extraordinary abstract design, form, motion, and theater.

Recently, I became involved with digital photography. I was never that interested in traditional film cameras and dark rooms. I don't really have a feel for the mechanical/chemical. I do have a feel for the digital/electronic. So, as soon as they were available, Rosalind and I gave ourselves a Christmas present of a Canon PowerShot G1, an Epson printer that can make prints up to 13x19, and PhotoShop, a marvelous software program in which you can manipulate images in the most incredible ways.

I had taken the camera on our trip to San Francisco, and I happened to have it in my computer case, so I grabbed it. My timing on the first few shots I took was way off. The thing about my camera is that you can't just push the shutter down and snap the picture. You have to hold the shutter down while it gets its focus, and then, after what seems like ten minutes, it takes the picture. In reality, there is only a slight delay between my action and the camera's response. But enough of one to throw my timing off. So I got a lot of pictures of empty pavements.

I began to experiment with timing. I had to snap the picture before the people walked into the set-up. After about twenty or so shots, I had my timing down. I took about fifteen interesting pictures, pictures that turned out exactly as I imagined them, capturing the motion, the abstract designs, the purple shadows against the yellow sunlight, some people rushing to get somewhere, a couple flirting, a lady on her way from shopping, a homeless person smoking a cigarette, a business man with an attaché case, a young person dressed in baggy pants and Hawaiian shirt. Each picture captured a moment of action, frozen in time. Each picture seemed to crystallize just the right moment, the one that was most dramatic, most compositional, most exciting.

This particular photo shoot put me into a different time zone. Each shot was both in the moment I snapped it and in a future when the camera responded. To accomplish my goal I had to live in two time zones.

When we create, we often live in at least two time zones: the present and the future. Through the present we have access to the future in ways that would otherwise be closed to us. Of course, structural tension positions a strategic relationship between the current time and the future. We are in two time zones when we are in structural tension.

Another Dimension Of Time

We often experience another dimension of time when we are in the throes of the creative process, what we might call the eternal, the everlasting, the timeless. Our focus is so intensely directed, our involvement so complete, that time seems suspended. The next time you look at the clock, hours have passed, but it seemed you began just a moment ago.

To experience the eternal, the everlasting, the timeless is to be in the presence of another dimension of life. For many, it is a form of intimacy with some higher expanse of existence, of Prana—the life-breath— of something Divine. For others, it is total concentration, total engagement, total spirit, energy, and intent. It is mystical without being esoteric, spiritual without being religious, at once normal and extraordinary.

Such types of experiences are never evoked by trying to evoke them. We must not make it our goal. It is a by-product, not a product. But, as we engage in the creative process, we find these timeless moments, and they change us and change our lives. From the present to the future through a door of timelessness, we penetrate, for the briefest moment, the great mystery of time.

An Artful Life

There's an old question that is often asked, "What makes art art?" Marcel Duchamp answered this question by taking a bicycle wheel, and designating it as sculpture. He then defined other ordinary objects as art. He called these pieces "readymades." Duchamp was a master of painting and sculpture. His notorious *Nude Descending a Staircase, No. 2* (1912) was the runaway hit of the early Twentieth Century.

So why did someone who could paint or sculpt anything he could imagine pick something out of a junkyard, put it in a gallery, and call it art? Because this particular bicycle wheel was art. Duchamp's vision could see beyond the ordinary to the essence of a thing. We usually ignore such observations in our rush to get someplace. But, as all visual artists have done, we can train our eye. More importantly, we can train our perception so that we can see what is there to see. Art creates universes in which we can live. As we watch a great film, we live in that universe. As we listen to a great rock song, we live in that universe. As we look at a bicycle wheel, we can live in that universe.

Each of these universes is unique unto itself. Each has its own governing principles, its own rhythms, its own sensibilities, and its own atmospheres. In our lives, we live in many universes. Some of them we create, others we visit. In some we may feel trapped. In others we feel joy, liberation, peace, or excitement. Who are we in these various universes? We can be the artist making the art. We can be Duchamp seeing the extraordinary in the commonplace.

Yet, Duchamp did more than call a bicycle wheel art. He changed the idea of what an artist is. He once bought a cheap reproduction of Leonardo da Vinci's *Mona Lisa* from a secondhand shop. He painted a mustache on it and signed it. Later, he bought another cheap reproduction of the *Mona Lisa* and signed it. He called the second one *Mona Lisa – shaved.* In one of his most famous iconoclastic remarks he said, "An artist is someone who signs things."

Of course, there is great comic theater in these antics. But there is a deeper insight too. That we make art by how we see. We make art by our definitions. We make art in more ways than making a painting, writing a script, composing music, and choreographing a dance. We make art by how we live our lives.

But art isn't just seeing something and calling it art. Duchamp wasn't being arbitrary. He was being very deliberate. He moved objects to new locations to be able to redefine them as art. He didn't imply everything is art wherever you look. He picked objects carefully, objects that had visual or programmatic interest. He was able to see art in places where often others would miss it. Art is not philosophy. It is an outcome of the creative process. It is the tangible manifestation of something very human, the dynamic urge to make something.

The something that we can make is our lives. We don't do this by simply calling our lives art. Duchamp took the bicycle wheel out of the junkyard and put it into a gallery, thus creating a stage for it. Was it the wheel, the stage, or his creative process that transformed the piece? It was all three, because they were inextricably tied together.

This book is not about calling your life art, and, therefore, hoping it will become more of what you want. It is about the principles that all artists must use to *produce* art. Through your actions, learning, imagination, desires, experimentation, observations, self-discipline, clarity, and work, you can transform your life. Only when your life becomes your creation, can you experience it as a work of art and experience yourself as its artist.

Is there a right way to live your life? No. You must create the way you live. You may create it unconsciously, haphazardly, without benefit of your own critical choices. When this is the case, there's a good chance you will not like what you have created.

If, however, you adopt the principles of the creative process as practiced in the arts, you will be more able to create your life as a sculptor shapes the stone, the composer develops the theme, the architect balances function, style, site, climate, materials, financing, and building codes.

You can invent your life with increasing mastery, in the same way artists always strive for greater and greater mastery over their creative process. There will be goals to achieve, but they are only a small part of the picture. The larger creation is found in your relationship with yourself, other people, your community, your world, and your universe. Your relationship with your own life can be identical to the relationship the painter has with the painting, the composer with the score, the architect to the building.

The mechanics, orientation, and spirit of the creative process, together, form the generative force that transforms a life, enriches it, fulfills it, makes it whole and involved, makes possible the deepest desires that the soul, mind, and spirit cherish. Your life as art.

We hope you have enjoyed this book and have found the concepts and principles of value. If you would like information about trainings in Robert Fritz's approach, structural consulting services, and products offered by Robert Fritz, Inc. you may reach us at:

Robert Fritz, Inc.
P.O. 116
Williamsville, Vt
05362-0116

Telephone:	(800) 848-9700
	(802) 348-7176
Fax:	(802) 348-7444
E-mail:	info@robertfritz.com

Also, visit our website to learn about Robert Fritz events, news, and schedules: www.robertfritz.com

A b o u t   t h e   A u t h o r

F or over the past twenty-five years, Robert Fritz has been developing the field of structural dynamics though his work, first in the area of the creative process, and then in the area of organizational, business, and management issues. He is the founder of *Technologies for Creating®, Inc., Robert Fritz, Inc.;* and *RJF Productions.*

Fritz began to lead courses in the creative process as applied to personal effectiveness in the mid-Seventies. He began to train others to lead his courses, and more than eighty-thousand people have participated in these trainings throughout the world.

His first major discovery was the *macrostructural pattern,* which describes the long range patterns in people's lives. While each individual's pattern was unique, he observed that there were two general types of patterns that people have: *oscillating,* and *resolving* or *advancing.* In the late Seventies, he began his work on two basic questions: why do these patterns exist and what does it take to change them form oscillating to resolving?

These questions led Fritz to pursue deeper questions about the structural make-up of human motivation. His first major book on the subject was *The Path of Least Resistance,* which quickly became a best seller. That was followed by his second book, *Creating.* These books, along with the TFC trainings have introduced revolutionary ideas about the influence of structural causality on human beings, both as individuals and within organizations. His organizational books, *Corporate Tides* and *The Path of Least Resistance for Managers,* have influenced managers, executive coaches, and organizations throughout the world.

In the early Eighties, Fritz began to teach consultants the principles of structure in a course called *The Fundamentals of Structural Consulting* (FSC). During the first few years of its existence, over two thousand people went through the FSC. But, the training did not really enable those people to become structural consultants. When Rosalind Hanneman became the London director of TFC-UK, she set out to learn how to master the structural consulting process. She began to transcribe demonstrations of structural consultations that Fritz would do during training sessions, and then study them until she could understand why each question was asked, and what insight it produced. She continued to practice the fundamental techniques she had learned by using them with her clients, and eventually, she began to master structural consulting. Sometime during this period, Fritz and Rosalind Hanneman fell in love, she moved to America, and they married. Rosalind—now Rosalind Fritz—developed the first comprehensive training program in structural consulting, and the first certification in structural consulting was awarded to those who were able to demonstrate professional and technical competence.

As a consultant, Robert Fritz helped many organizations put the structural approach into practice, and his clients include several Fortune 500 companies, many mid-size companies, as well as governmental and non-profit organizations. Working with other structural consultants, *Robert Fritz, Inc.* is in the forefront of a revolutionary change in how organizations structure themselves to produce sustained high performance.

Fritz began the study of structure as a composition student at the Boston Conservatory of Music in the Sixties. Later, he studied composition in Germany, and was on the faculty of New England Conservatory of Music, and Berklee College. After receiving his BM and MM in composition, Frtiz worked as a studio musician in New York and Hollywood, and won positions in *Playboy* and *Downbeat* magazine readers' polls. Fritz is still an active composer, and has written film scores, operas, symphonic and chamber music. Most recently, Fritz also has been writing and directing films. Both he and Rosalind have hosted the TV series *Creating*. He is currently a member of the board of directors of the Brattleboro Museum and Art Center.

Robert and Rosalind Fritz live in Vermont with their seventeen-year-old daughter, Eve.